ACTIVATE JOY

LIVE YOUR LIFE
BEYOND
LIMITATIONS

ACTIVATE JOY

LIVE YOUR LIFE
BEYOND
LIMITATIONS

BY

ALIXSANDRA PARNESS, DD

NEW PAGE BOOKS
A division of The Career Press, Inc.
Pompton Plains, NJ

ACTIVATE JOY
EDITED AND TYPESET BY NICOLE DeFELICE
Cover design by Joseph Sherman/Dutton & Sherman Design
Printed in the U.S.A.

To order this title, please call toll-free 1-800-CAREER-1 (NJ and Canada: 201-848-0310) to order using VISA or MasterCard, or for further information on books from Career Press.

The Career Press, Inc.
220 West Parkway, Unit 12
Pompton Plains, NJ 07444
www.careerpress.com
www.newpagebooks.com

Library of Congress Cataloging-in-Publication Data
Parness, AlixSandra.
    Activate joy : live your life beyond limitations / by AlixSandra Parness.
        p. cm.
    Includes index.
    ISBN 978-1-60163-213-5 -- ISBN 978-1-60163-602-7 (ebook) 1. Joy. 2. Self-realization. 3. Spiritual life. I. Title.

    BF575.H27P374 2012
    152.4'2--dc23

                                                        2011045930

Dedicated to Lee,
forever in the light.

BLESSINGS AND APPRECIATIONS

My blessings and appreciations enfold the people who have made my dream of healing the heart of humanity, one heart at a time, a reality. First and foremost, my husband, Lee; my devoted support, the love of my life, the blessing that allowed for the spiritual awakening within me. My joy partner of more than 40 years, the father of my children, and the blessing of unconditional love in my life, Lee blesses me still from the realm of non-physical and guides my path with his unconditional love that is with me always. My eternal blessings to my three children who have supported and cheered me on all these many years. You are each a diamond in my treasure chest and when I think of you, I sparkle with delight.

I appreciate and bless my close circle of teachers who believed in the teachings and have added their voices and love, continually expanding all that we are. I appreciate all of those who call themselves students who found their way into my sphere of light and love, learned from me, and took the teaching out into their world. I call you teachers, uplifters, and healers, Divine Masters of the first order, and I bless our eternal connection always.

Life lived is a treasure chest filled with gems, jewels, pearls, sparkling diamonds, and soft downy puffs of light. We begin to gently save our treasures year after year, the newest ones being closest to the top. Sometimes, on a rainy day, we might venture into that secret place only we know about, just to see what we have stored away. Then we sift and sort our treasures, recalling the empowering moments shared.

Writing this book has been like that for me. Waking up in the early morning with a new idea or vantage point for clarification while writing this book requires reaching into my treasure chest of blessings to recall the people and the circumstances that activated my joy.

As I feel into the many layers of wisdom gained from years of seeking and allowing, I must say thank you to Jane Roberts and Rob Butts for *The Seth Material.* Each pearl on the strands of enlightenment Seth gave all of us would not have been as bright without the eternal wisdom I gained in those years. The luster of my life was realized through those teachings. As I attend the Abraham gatherings these days, Esther and Jerry Hicks feel like the more expanded version of those original teachings. My blessings and appreciations are deep and heart-felt for these beautiful people. I value the empowerment being spun into the fabric of humanity and want to continue to add to my song as well.

I will discuss a little about Ouna and my dolphin experience. This was in 1984 when she (Ouna) was teaching me about the multidimensional levels of the chakra systems. I had never even really understood the importance of chakras up to that point. I was in ministerial training learning about God and the Bible. This understanding that was evolving into the me I am today would lead me five years later into the Barbara Brennan School of Healing located in East Hampton, New York. My blessings and appreciations are boundless, as I learned so much in those years about chakras and the energetic body. I was also very fortunate to have been with Barbara in the first two years she opened her school in East Hampton. In fact, I was with each of my teachers as they embarked on their new expanded teachings, hmmmm. We owned a summer home in Hampton Bays for many years, and that was really a power place for me, my husband, and my children to grow and play. Those years with Barbara Brennan were life-changing and expansive as I had already experienced a natural ability to transmit healing energy several years before.

My life was expanding rapidly and in different directions when a new teacher, Dr. Robert Jaffe, came into my church. Dr. Jaffe was just awakening to a new teaching, which he offered to us. We became friends and I later worked with him and taught with him in Sedona, Arizona, and Europe. I often referred to him lovingly as my "Blue Jean Buddha." So you can see my treasure chest is rich and deep with blessings from these wise and generous people.

In 1980, I was introduced to Marcos Orbito, a Filipino psychic surgeon who was to change the course of my life and the life of Lee, my husband. During the course of two years, I traveled with him and witnessed the phenomenon of true psychic surgery. These experiences were needed for the foundation of my understanding that all illness begins and ends with our thought-filled belief systems. Recently I heard Abraham, channeled through Esther Hicks, say that "no one chooses disease for any reason; we allow [or accept] it by default." It is time for us to change that old and worn-out flawed premise. The change that is to come is to deliberately choose health and well-being by aligning with our value and worth and trusting that this awareness is truly so. I am so appreciative of this experience because, through my personal witnessing of hundreds of people in many circumstances of disease, I know that how you think and feel about how you think attracts the reality you live.

My dearest friend and artist Rachael, now passed, befriended me when I first moved to Las Vegas in 1976. We met in Temple Ner Tamid where Lee and I chose to attend services. Rachel and I were always learning and searching for new and exciting things to explore. She called me one day to tell me about a channel coming to town who spoke for an extraterrestrial named Bashar. The five years we traveled to California or the Flamingo Library in Las Vegas to listen to this astounding information will enrich me for the rest of my eternal life. Rachel and I took the first groups to swim with the dolphins in Key Largo. We laughed all the time. I deeply appreciated her unconditionally loving friendship, her amazing insights, and her beautiful self. She blesses me still.

This book has been written and rewritten within the chambers of my heart for many years now. *Activate Joy* became a reality when I decided to write about my journey in this life. As soon as that decision was made and the first words appeared on the page, these words soon filled 20 pages. I called Janet Reed, who had attended only one Inner Focus workshop, and had offered her services as an editor should I ever need her. She was a wonderful blessing and through her help gave me the courage to continue on. Thank you.

I then called on a dear friend and my graphic designer for years, Rebecca Fisher, lovingly known as Becca. She helped me create the first prototype of this book. I am blessed to have her in my life, as we have a deep bond between us and I treasure her ability to translate my visions into graphic works of art.

You have experienced the expansion of a dream, I am sure. Writing a book is daunting and very scary, as the publishing industry has changed radically. As I write these words, they cannot adequately describe my appreciation for my newfound friends and publishing co-creators, Ja-lene Clark and Jo Ann Deck of GatherInsight.com. To me, this book is a work of art because of the love and dedication the three of us found in one another. We have all been changed and expanded through the developmental process of editing, changing, and exchanging ideas, swimming in the sea of creativity together, and basking in the sheer joy of bringing the completed work to press. My blessings and appreciations enfold these beautiful people. I felt the soft hands of all of those I have mentioned offering me their blessing, cheering me on, and I knew I had done well.

And now I share my appreciations with Michael and Laurie Pye and my friends at New Page Books. Because of their support, *Activate Joy* will now be distributed to the larger world. My appreciations are deep and ever flowing; thank you all.

To all of you reading these words, I invite you to go beyond the words into the deep feelings of what is being offered here. Take this teaching and make it yours; live it, and then offer your experience to those who are waiting for you to share your wisdom.

In the Silence of the Rain

by AlixSandra Parness

In the Silence of the Rain
I can feel the pain inside; I can let my silent tears,
Wash away my willful pride and lift my broken heart.

In the Silence of the Rain
I can hold myself and cry, for all the loving moments I've allowed to pass
me by.
I can let those silent tears wash away my willful pride,
and soften my hardened heart.

In the Silence of the Rain
I can learn to forgive all those who've caused me pain, especially me.
I can feel the silent tears wash away my willful pride
and heal my wounded heart.

In the Silence of the Rain
I stand naked—washed clean before the day,
approaching now the threshold of this moment—
I vow to
face my beauty,
shine my magnificence,
bring my soul fully into my life.
I realize at this moment
I have chosen to open my loving heart,
and now, I live today
in the ecstasy of beauty and joy.

and rest in my silent joy,
After the Rain.

CONTENTS

Preface

Awakening

Follow me, let me share the joy of the fast-moving waters, sleeking my friends as they swim by. I live a life of limitless joy and so can you.
—The Dolphins

This book is dedicated to the awakening of humanity in our lifetime, awakening to the silver cord that has always connected us to our personal source of All That Is. And so, I invite you to take a personal journey with me as I recount how I awakened into being truly able to love myself and allowing joy to always light my way.

When I think of joy, I think of my friends the dolphins and the frequency of joy they bring into our world. For me, it was the dolphins that awakened me and helped me understand my true multidimensional nature. Through many years of channeling a dolphin I called Ouna, I learned about the energetic system of our physical bodies we call the chakra system. She awakened ancient knowledge and infinite wisdom that became the foundation for much of what I would teach in later years.

Being with the dolphins was not to become my life's work as I had once thought. Although for many years I took groups to swim with them in various parts of the world, my last trip was to say farewell to my joy partner in life, my husband, Lee.

I always connected easily to Ouna, but after channeling her for five years, one day her energy was not present. Several weeks later, in the company of a few friends, I had a visitation from her. She was not in dolphin form; rather she looked like a brilliant moving shaft of sparkling light. As she moved into my aura, I was lifted out of my body and tears brimmed in my eyes as she softly spoke to me. She came to thank me for allowing her a voice. She was deeply appreciative that I had taken her information and incorporated it in my healing practice, that I had indeed valued her and her wisdom. She told me that because of our experience together, she had ascended in her own consciousness and was now a goddess of light.

I remember sitting on Jane Roberts's couch that first night in Elmira and literally feeling the vibration change as Seth began to speak. There was a confidence, a direct purpose in the words being spoken, I felt thrilled and excited all at the same time. That room was filled with people who came together to seek the same thing—connection to something they thought was bigger than self—and in the process revealed authentic self-love.

Jane worked very diligently to make sure that the words and ideas being expressed through her were authentic, and I deeply respect that. Because of her impeccable attention to the source of her information, her example paved my future as a conscious channel, allowing me to experience the benefits of clear channeling. The transmissions I received through Jane and Seth are still present, expanded now because I have embodied the teachings and therefore live them.

After Seth I found Bashar, an extraterrestrial group of beings channeled through Darryl Anka. During the five years I attended the Bashar sessions, the messages were a little different from those received through Jane; however, the essential ingredient of unconditional love remained consistent. If I were to pick one idea from Seth that still moves me today, it would be the opening remarks in the book *Seth Speaks*: **You create your own reality.** From Bashar, it is his classic statement that we are **masters of limitation** and civilizations from all over the galaxies are watching to see how far we will expand once we let go. And, I must admit, so am I.

Now Abraham-Hicks is on the scene with one constant message that is shaking up the status quo and leading the way. Because I believe that our time has come, I see Abraham cheering us on. I can almost hear a chorus of "hip-hip-hoorah, here comes Abraham to tip the scale!" This book was able to be written with such grace because I caught the love ball from Abraham, stacked it up with all the others I had in my treasure chest and let go of my self-imposed limiting beliefs. I give myself permission to be a voice for freedom and use the language of my life experience to deliver it.

We are all in a process of awakening to a greater light that beams from the heart of who we are—ascending, expanding with the wisdom gained, and transmitting and activating the joy with which we came into this life. I want to dedicate this book to the joyous hearts of the dolphins that are an intricate part of who we truly are. "Follow me," they say, "let me share the joy of the fast-moving waters, sleeking my friends as they swim by. I live a life of limitless joy and so can you."

Then, as *Activate Joy* was completed, and before it could expand into an even greater tool of awakening, the horses pranced gently into my life. A dear friend of mine and graduate of the Inner Focus School had created a magnificent horse farm called Spirit Gate where she rescues and allows these spiritually advanced beings an opportunity to express their true nature in a dance of equine equality, and I was honored to take part in this adventure. Hero, the leader of the herd, began to speak to me, and this continued for many days. He told me of a place in the galaxies where horse consciousness reigns supreme and explained that well-being was the order of this universe. He introduced himself as the shaman of the herd. One of the geldings had a swollen knee and eye infection, and Hero and I worked as a team to heal him. Hero said, "I am shaman. If you come to me first, we can work together in harmony to quicken the gelding's healing process." I was transported into another world with a deep awareness of the infinite intelligence of All That Is.

Even after writing this book, my blessings continue as I awaken to living in a consistent state of joy. Beyond limitations, I find that unconditional love expands me beyond myself, over and over again. I know firsthand that as each of us accepts and allows the possibilities of living our life beyond limitations, the vistas are neverending and the joy is boundless. Now, I can give this blessing and pass it along to you as you read these words and embody the teachings therein. Thank You.

Chapter 1

Being Joyful

Think of something that makes you smile.

When we are little children, there is joy in everything. The amazing things of life continuously present reasons for us to be joyful. Joy is dancing in the air within the sunbeams coming through the window. You can see all sorts of marvelous things in those little gleaming lights. It is as if the smiling sun welcomes you into this fantastic human playground. There is joy in being hugged, touched, and loved as you reach out to experience the world. You can smell the sweetness of mom when she enters your room, and feel joy when you hear the coo of her voice as she reaches out for you. Then there is the pleasure of eating, and that particular pleasure of taste that continues to be a real delight for almost all of us.

OODLES OF JOY

I married at 18; my first child was born within a year. Vividly, I remember one evening several years later when my brother, his wife, and their son came over for dinner. I made spaghetti and put the kids at a small table in my daughter's room just off the kitchen. The adults sat in the dining area, out of the children's sight, but not out of earshot. We talked, enjoying our meal, and listened to the kids giggle.

I thought I should go in to see what all the fun was about and, to my surprise, when I walked into the room, there was spaghetti everywhere. Those cute little hands had used sauce and noodles to finger paint the walls and the table. There was spaghetti on the little chairs they were delightfully wiggling on. But the cutest sight was the overturned bowls of noodles hanging upside down on their little heads. They were in such joy. Neither of the kids noticed us, but when they did, the laughter and giggles stopped.

There was stillness and silence as the kids awaited their fate, breathing on hold, mouths dropped. The *oh no* looks on their little faces absolutely stopped me in my tracks. What did the children think would happen? My brother had stepped in behind me. The kids' eyes were as wide as saucers. Just a few moments passed, and my brother and I laughed so hard, we cried. When the kids saw our reaction, after they started to breathe again, they laughed along with us. I have never seen and felt such unbridled joy!

To activate joy is such a simple effort and one worth doing as often as you think about it. Think of something that makes you smile and gives you a warm feeling all over, perhaps a memory that brings you into a happy place for a time, that paves the way for future moments of alignment. We are born aligned and activated to joy. Now, it is just a short reach of allowing to give it a place in our lives once again.

Inspired By the Blooms

Joy is experienced in all of our senses. Another way I can activate joy is by remembering the smell of freshly mown grass, or walking along a path and smelling flowers. I loved to pick flowers as a child. In my mind there were no boundaries, no limitations, and no fences worth paying any attention to that could keep me from the flowers. Flowers spoke to me; they were kissed by the sunbeams I remembered streaming through the window onto my wall. And have I told you how much I love the rain? If Mom didn't watch me closely, I would wander out the kitchen door when it rained, just to stand in awe of what was falling from the sky. Where did those things come from? If I stuck my tongue out, the drops tickled me, and felt good on my face. I had no fear of thunder or lightning, and in Vestal, New York, the thunder really crackled and roared. There is sheer joy in my heart as I recall the awesomeness of it all.

Flowers so inspired me, especially tulips, because they looked like little cups for my tea parties. It never mattered to me where they were, I just wanted to pick them. My neighbors knew that when I was walking, my mission was to bring my mom a bouquet of flowers. Sometimes Marion up the street would poke her head out of the door and say, "Sandra, don't pull up the roots now, pick them gently. Take just a few today; we need to leave some for the fairies to dance around tonight." As I think back on those warm spring days from my childhood, I am grateful for the blessing of our lovely neighbors. I often wondered if Marion could also hear the sunbeams calling to her. Somehow all the ladies around us found joy in seeing a little girl who loved their tulips so much, knowing the flowers would grace my mom's table that afternoon.

REAWAKEN JOY

Take a moment and recall the active joy in your childhood. Even if your childhood had stretches of challenges or trauma, as mine did, you can always reach deep and find a positive experience to reflect on because joy follows you wherever you go—you just can't help it. Allow these feelings of well-being and celebration to wash over you. Know that as you allow these or any other good feelings to emerge, you are deliberately aligning yourself with joy. As you reawaken this most natural part of you, let yourself bask in the freedom of that young mind. Relive the joy of running. That was something, wasn't it? Running, swinging, riding that Big Wheel, feeling the breeze on your face and in your hair. Oops, falling! Well, that was part of running. We always fell.

The tumble was followed by the sound of Mom or Dad rushing over to see if we were hurt. I always cried harder when I saw them coming because I just loved the fuss they made over me. Joy echoed in my heart at the sound of their concern, the softness of their voices, even the quiet chiding about running, and falling down—all blending into the sound of love.

We *can* reach back into our happy memories to reawaken and activate the innocent joy we once knew. It's interesting to realize that once these pictures begin to bubble to the surface, there are more to come. Joy begets joy.

I remember one Christmas morning after all the packages were opened, Mom and Dad upstairs having a rest, I—Grandma—just putting the cinnamon rolls in the oven for breakfast later. It was just too quiet so I tiptoed into my bedroom area to see where my granddaughters were. Basking in the joy of the morning's festivities, I stood for a long time outside my closed door listening to my darling little ones' soft giggles and gentle talking. I opened the door and peeked inside. They were sitting on the floor, licking the huge lollypops I had given them on top of their presents, sticky red stuff all over their faces. They looked up and smiled, inviting me into their vortex of joy. As I joined them and relished in the happiness of children's delight, I was transported back into the spaghetti scene from years ago. While sitting there I made a conscious, deliberate choice to activate joy anytime, for no reason at all, just the way children do all the time.

This book is here to serve you, to remind you of what you once knew, and to bring you to a new level of conscious awareness and deliberate choice. Come with me and we will explore ideas, my personal journey, and the places we get stuck, and

I will give you tools to help you activate joy so that you may become as you intended: a deliberate creator of joy in this extraordinary world.

CHAPTER 2

FINDING YOUR JOY

IF JOY WERE A POINT ON THE COMPASS, IT WOULD
POINT THE WAY TO HAPPINESS AND FULFILLMENT.

When something excites you and you feel good about it, follow it as far as you can to see where it leads. Excitement breeds the energy of passion. As these good feelings continue to be a part of your process, thoughts form around the feelings, creating a belief pattern. The full-blown pattern, the combination of the tone of your feelings, your mood, and your beliefs, resonates and becomes your point of attraction. Your natural creative spirit has already replaced patterns that are worn out and no longer work for you with new, fresh ideas. All you have to do is allow an attitude of joy to flow into your life.

Joy Flow Forumla

Excitement and good feelings create
the energy of passion.

Passion creates new
thought forms.

Thought forms create attitude.

Attitude is your point of attraction
that brings forth your experience.

ALIGN WITH WHAT YOU WANT

When or if we align with the positive feelings associated with joy, we move toward finding our joy. Aligning is important. By first aligning with what you want, you will get where you want to go much faster. Most of us have spent a lifetime pouring energy into healing old hurts and traumas. I believe those were necessary steps in truly knowing what we do not want in our lives. From those healings, many of us, myself included, emerged with a more refined consciousness and became more aware and deliberate in the choices we are making today. Seeing those old hurts and traumas in a new light has certainly helped in realizing our true worthiness. **This book is deliberately focused on fearlessly moving into levels beyond our present understanding to find and help us live with joy activated in every area of our life. This fearless focus is something that I am extraordinarily diligent about every day.**

I have been given many new techniques and processes that my students and I use to activate joy. These teachings include learning to tame those voices of fear and uncertainties (I call them your Yabbits—"yeah-buts"), the Basking Process, the Art of Blessing, the Goodness Process, and being debt-free. Together my students and I have been on a journey to replace worn beliefs with the knowledge that we are the essence of pure goodness, that we don't owe anything to anyone, and we deliberately and consciously choose to value ourselves. You will learn these ways to live your life beyond limitations and align with joy.

WHEN BELIEFS BATTLE THE BODY

"My health was very poor at the time I decided to attend the Inner Focus School. Feeling happy was not at all easy. I would have settled for one day of feeling good. At that time, I had lost 20 percent of my body weight and I was in a physical and emotional crisis. I didn't understand what was happening to me. I tried so many things to find relief and I was tired of trying. I felt like I wanted to die. I simply didn't know what to do. I was scared."

Andra had been to many practitioners, but none could give her relief. The thought that no one could help her was overwhelming. She also had digestive issues. Her muscles were taut all the time, she was visibly clenched up, afraid of the world and everything in it. She had left the corporate world, believing her health issues were related to job stress. When she came to an Inner Focus class (my school in Las Vegas) for the first time, she didn't know if she could make it through the day. She was weak and needed to eat and sleep every few hours. Working together for a short time, she realized that her mind would obsess about things, especially negative experiences or worries about her health. Strongly embedded negative patterns held her tight. She truly believed that there was something wrong with her, that she was unlovable, that her life had no value, and that she was small and insignificant. These beliefs were visibly reflected on her body.

As her healing progressed, she learned to discern the voices inside her of the perfectionist, the critic, and the commentator. These "Yabbits" were her point of attraction, running her life, and keeping her trapped in fear. Each new awareness lifted Andra out of the deep despair that had become her life and she showed greater and greater strides in allowing the true light of her higher self into the forefront of her life. Later she told me,

"I didn't know that I was missing something. My life lacked so much…beauty, love, peace, mystery, adventure, joy…" She wrote me a note that is close to my heart. "The tools that I have learned from you, AlixSandra, have been invaluable. They support me in increasing my awareness of who I am. They also give me the confidence that I can know anything about myself and change whenever I desire. As a result of my determination to live, I have been able to free myself pretty much from limitations. And I am so much happier!"

As I watch others move beyond very challenging obstacles, I know that finding joy is possible, even in the most extreme circumstances. For myself, I now fully accept the parts of the activate joy puzzle I had been missing.

I absolutely now know and accept that:

- ❧ I am an eternal being having a physical experience.

- ❧ I am okay and there is nothing I need to prove to anyone, because my worthiness is a given truth.

- ❧ Everything is within me. Free choice allows me to choose my expression, no matter in which direction I want to go.

- ❧ Everyone else is okay just the way they are.

- ❧ Limiting or painful experiences that have already manifested in my life are irrelevant to who I am right now.

- ❧ Joy is the essence of my life purpose, and following my joy *is* my only purpose.

Whenever I read that list, I feel a thousand pounds lighter. I now realize the extent of the debt I incurred by denying the greater part of me all these years. That is what had been missing. When I feel these words come alive within me, I am in a hot air balloon, and each statement is a weight that drops away, allowing me to align with my True Self, that part of me that loves me unconditionally. Eyes of appreciation watch me unfold as I rise to the occasion of my enlightenment again and again. Softly, joy enters my heart each time I see the world from a higher perspective than ever before. I can see more clearly now through the eyes of my greater self.

WHAT DO YOU DO WITH UNCOMFORTABLE FEELINGS?

I had a revelation just a few months ago during the graduation week of the Inner Focus School. During the years of creating the Inner Focus community, I had become so attached to the name "Inner Focus" that I lost sight of myself…My dearest friend was appreciating the Inner Focus program, and all she had learned and discovered about herself through the teachings. After hearing her go on and on, I started to feel uncomfortable. Even though we were close friends, my name was not mentioned once. Old teachings might suggest my feelings were just an ego rush, and I should tuck them away, ignore them, or keep them somewhere out of sight. After all, I had become a master at that.

Now I know differently. Those uncomfortable feelings were pointing me toward a new acceptance. Once I realized this, I knew it was a major turning point for me because I could accept and easily go with the flow. When my turn came to speak in the circle, I stood up and stated, "I Am AlixSandra, Divine Master. Inner Focus is what I do, it is not who I am."

Dive into uncharted waters and be willing to look honestly at your true feelings. You might see that if you falsely think another is deliberately doing something to hurt you, you could be stuck in a whirlpool of self-doubt. On the other hand, by taking responsibility for your own feelings, you rise up and speak for what you truly want.

Joy emerged from within my uncomfortable feelings about what was being said, that my own particular contribution was not mentioned. Without judgment, as I allowed my inner worthiness a voice, I freed myself from years of bondage I had inflicted upon myself. The acceptance rose when I valued myself enough to claim a higher truth.

The reason this book is now in print is because another close friend told me I had to write about me. Until that moment when he showed me that truth, I had writer's block. I had thought that I needed to write something different, more in the direction of the Inner Focus School. I had to value the fact that first there was me and my experiences, and then came Inner Focus. Subtle difference, isn't it? However, that awareness was life-changing.

JOY IS THE ANSWER

I have been a pastor, teacher, and mentor for more than 25 years. I have met with people all over the world, listening to their needs and desires, helping them find answers, and watching the transformations that took place. In all this, I have learned that life can be distilled into three short phrases:

Find your joy.

Live in joy.

Give others the same opportunity.

Being in joy is so simple, isn't it? So why aren't we doing it? Why is unfettered success eluding us? Why is there still suffering? Why are we so disconnected from one another?

Joy is what we are all seeking. Most of us have no idea the secret is that simple because life has caused us to create self-limiting boundaries, and to adhere to the rules and man-made laws of the day. This deactivates our joy, replacing it with hard work, determination, comparison, sadness, and depression. Those feelings have consequences such as disease, misalignment, unhappiness, and often despair. Have you also noticed that when your focus is targeted on something unpleasant, it tends to grow larger and larger in your life experience?

Now, when we focus on something that feels like passion, it also gains momentum. The Law of Attraction, which we will also explore, does not discriminate. Excitement and passion are like doors opening to greater awareness. When one door is opened, that leads to more doors and to shiny rooms that are filled with exciting new ideas and rays of inspiration. The operative word here is *excitement*. Our emotions clearly indicate which side of the fence we are standing on. Excitement and passion tell a story that must be acknowledged. If joy were a point on the compass, it would point the way to happiness and fulfillment. As I continue to build a consciousness, which whole-heartedly believes in my own worthiness and trusts that the universe I choose to be a part of will give me everything and anything I want, I am ready to receive *more* happiness. I want more love. I want more unconditional joy. I imagine that you share these same feelings with me.

LOOKING FOR LOVE AND JOY IN ALL THE WRONG PLACES

It seems as if, in my generation, "spare the rod and spoil the child" was an accepted and preferred method for parenting. Parents really believed that punishment and holding a hard line would benefit their children and help them become better adults.

In a new Inner Focus group in the Midwest, one student was beautiful, with a powerful, put-together presence. As she sat in the front row, I would never have guessed the abuse she had endured throughout her life.

Amanda was sexually abused as a very young child. She could only find relief when she was alone, and so set a pattern of attracting men who were emotionally distant. When we worked together in class, she had a hard time speaking in front of anyone. She had an overriding fear that she was never going to get it right, so she would not talk at all. As Amanda was dedicated to healing and as she continued on her path, she wanted to have a successful relationship, but found that she attracted men who had very low self-esteem, and who eventually became both verbally and physically abusive.

I remember a powerful session in which she had a realization that she believed that to be loved it had to be painful. In this session, we did the Goodness Process, one of my major teachings, and it unearthed her belief system. After this session, she began to record her life experiences and moved to the southwest, determined to find joy and live a happier life. Ultimately, she sifted through one more unhappy relationship before she let her gentle spirit out and attracted the love of her life. Amanda found out that finding joy requires allowing joy in.

You have to be willing to redirect your attention away from the abuse patterns to allow hope to blossom and invite better experiences. Amanda realized she *was* a worthy, deserving person. When there is hope, a new vision evolves, and those painful memories dissolve when you reach for happiness. She told me, "When I finally came to the realization that *I did not want* any more abusive relationships in my life, everything shifted. I felt solid and powerful and very happy being me. This determination opened the door for Joe, buying a ranch, and the horses who have been my teachers, to come in." Her new horse Sunny was a wonderful Palomino whose spirit had been broken through years of being tied down. "Sunny is just looking for freedom and love," she told me. "Similar to me, I always felt tied up and confined and now I have love. I have freedom to be me."

As I look into the world these days, the expanded consciousness is apparent. We are recognizing the absolute need for positive self-esteem and less need for the rod. We are learning to bless and praise rather than yell, cuss, and condemn. Young parents want what parents have wanted forever—something better for their children than they had. One generation lights the next and the next and the next until all the world is light.

GROUP JOY

Several years ago, I became interested in the 2012 Alignment occurring on December 21, 2012. On the Internet, there is an abundance of information from people on what they think will happen in 2012. So I went to the accepted authority on the Mayan Calendar, José Argüelles. Because of his expertise on the subject, he seemed capable of giving valuable information on how this ancient culture held the secrets of this time in their future. The Mayan Calendar stops on that fateful date, and then we don't know what comes after. Naturally, being humans with avid love for high drama, collectively we decide it must be catastrophic.

The 2012 Alignment will bring our Milky Way, our sun and our Earth, into an alignment that only happens every 26,000 years (say the experts). Because we have no idea why, but realize the significance, we speculate, we get scared, and we make up stories to suit the needs of the voices of fear and uncertainties inside us. Now, as kids, we loved to be scared; that was exciting, but most of the excitement was in the chase or making faces at one another. These antics all ended in peals of unending laughter. We instinctively knew that joy was in everything and we were too smart to be scared for real. The older we got, the more we believed in all things scary, and we learned to make up stories that seem so real that we actually believe them.

I knew in my heart that 2012 *really* represented a very different alignment. Even the ancient Maya had no symbols to describe this time. Some people do say that 2012 and beyond will be apocalyptic and devastating. When I first heard that disaster scenario, I reflected back on how worried people were about the coming of the millennium in the year 2000. Some people went to extreme measures to protect themselves from that manmade idea, about which they had no personal knowledge, but faithfully followed the prophecies of fear. Of course there were the expert voices revving up the scene…and as I recall nothing happened, but it sure made good television.

Reaching back in my experience, I am reminded of what happened on a New Year's Eve at Hamm Hall on the Las Vegas campus of the University of Nevada. I spent that entire year organizing a city-wide event around an idea that John Randolph Price wrote about in his book *The Planetary Commission*. The idea was to connect with people all over the world and join together for a moment of Prayer for Peace on December 31, 1986, at 12:00 Greenwich Mean Time. In cities and countries from Russia to Australia, the idea was like a groundswell that just kept growing. In our town, all of the various spiritual communities gathered at 6 p.m. that day to take part in an exciting "Peace Expo." Booths and tables were set up to show what everyone was doing to further the much-desired consciousness of peace. People brought musical offerings and talked to one another. There was hope; there was joy; there was expectation; there was innocence. There was camaraderie and a sharing I have not seen since. I am here to tell you that joy was present then, bouncing up and down. You could feel it in full force that night.

Starting at midnight, the Las Vegas strip stars began to arrive for the celebration and offered a concert of great magnitude. No one cared if the 4,000 seats in Hamm Hall were filled; we sang for the sheer joy of knowing that we were all a part of something extraordinary and greater than ourselves. None of us knew exactly what, but we knew it felt grand. The countdown was electric. There we were, candles lit, singing "One Lights Another," written by Candace Coar. As news came in from Hawaii, Russia, France, Israel, and South America, we raised our light even higher. Consciousness all over the world connected with one shared goal: world peace. As one person, I knew I had made a difference.

COLLECTIVE PARADIGM SHIFT

The promise of a shift in the consciousness such as this is magnetic. Sometimes without even knowing why, people were drawn in. Perhaps it was the hope or the responsibility that we all felt about being a part of creating a better world. My passion was ignited as I began to realize the joy of oneness that night. The vision shown to me as I stood before this wondrous crowd would pave my path with gold, and Inner Focus would be born a few years later. Looking back, I now recognize the paradigm shift that occurred within the heart of humanity in that instant. We stood at the doorway of a new level of consciousness and sang our way in. Everyone focused on one peaceful thought in the vortex of love and light.

To me, peace is not quiet; peace is alive and effervescent. Peace is allowing peace without trying to control it by wanting others to think and act the way you think they should, to fit into your idea of how you think things "should" be. Peace contains active joy because peace is a vortex of happiness, the happiness of freedom.

For me, 2012 is another moment like the one experienced during the Prayer for Peace, and the evidence of this has shown up everywhere. Another groundswell of people with expanding consciousness is looking for joy in their lives. There is a movement so great that is centered within us, creating an amplification effect that is tipping the scales in favor of more joy, which in its turn brings about peace and freedom. In 1986, we were looking to one another to make peace happen. In the new paradigm, we will understand the power of our own deliberate creation, individuals creating prosperity and happiness, attracting abundance and good health deliberately rather than by default.

Joy is present *right now*. Joy is *in* everything you do. Joy is beckoning you; magnetically guiding you into its vortex of happiness, passion, and peace. A natural alignment of galactic, universal, and personal consciousness will lead us to the joyous life we came here to live.

Now, how do you find this seemingly elusive joy?

1. **Believe** it is there.

2. **Start** with something you already feel joyful about.

3. **Ask** for joy to show itself to you.

Could joy be under a bowl of spaghetti atop a child's little head? Could it be in a song or the wagging of a puppy's tail? Could it be in a bouquet of tulips? Could it be in the kneading of a kitten's paws in your lap or the gallop of a beautiful horse? Could it be under that pile of dishes waiting for you in the sink, or along the produce aisle in the grocery store, or in the pleading eyes of those homeless people in the park? Use your imagination. What do you see? Could it be hiding behind pain from health challenges? Or waiting for you to release a child-hood trauma so you can experience happiness? Joy is magnetic; it creates its own force field. Joy will come to you and draw you in if you let it.

My journey is your journey. They may have different faces, be in different places, and yours are uniquely yours, but we both have the same intent: to find happiness and live joyously, *to turn away from ideas and thoughts that don't work and have never worked*, to deliberately create the experience only you can imagine for yourself. In the future, we will discover that there is a science to imagination because imagination fosters the awakening of a new and better world consciousness, not only for us, but also for future generations. Schools will teach a different curriculum, and children will feel the excitement of learning to focus and bring forth inspiration from their imaginations. This book is intended to open ideas for a new world of deliberate creators who value themselves and know their worthiness. Only then can true peace be allowed and known.

CHAPTER 3

JOY LOST

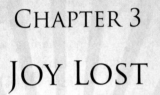

YOUR LOVE WILL BE WITH YOU ALL THE TIME, ALWAYS.

Lee was my husband, the father of my three children, and the love of my life, and we were married for many years. Our life was delicious and filled with family, excitement, travel, shared interests, and the sheer enjoyment of all things wonderful.

Just after attending our son's wedding, we learned that Lee had melanoma, and it had spread into his lymph nodes. In the few months that followed, we reached deliberately for things that would improve his health, such as foods that would boost his immune system, breathing patterns that would allow for a greater flow of oxygen, and even alternative wellness practices such as acupuncture. Lee remained filled with hope and a determined unwillingness to accept the fate that the doctors put upon him. He had survived a bad heart diagnosis with the help of a psychic surgeon some years earlier, and there was a positive belief pattern already in place. Despite his determination and all of my prayers, Lee left this reality eight months later in April 2001. My mother had passed just two months before Lee, so it was a very challenging time. I do know firsthand how hard it can be to find joy in your life when you are focused on things that are missing and grieving for what could have been.

GOOD GRIEF

As I write this book about joy, I am remembering my husband and knowing that it is so important to address the *perceived* loss of joy. Emotions play a major role in learning to deliberately create the new world we all envision. The emotions that emerge from loss are powerful and must also be recognized, appreciated, allowed, and understood.

As I struggle with the right words, and dive deep into myself to retrieve my true emotions, I actually feel both loss and excitement at the same time. For me, the loss was devastating. The despair I encountered was a bottomless pit that swirled around me constantly, keeping me within its grip far too long. I really learned the art of *dis-pair*—the distancing of the pair we were, the dis-connection of my world and all I knew it to be, and at that time I thought I could not, and did not want to go on. I missed him and the life we had built together, and in the missing place of limitation, my vision was dimmed.

Grief counselors talked to me about the cycles I would go through, including rage. And when rage loomed in front of me, I realized that it was rage aimed at myself for feeling as if I was not enough. Falsely I thought, "If I had done things differently, he would not have left." The vibrational hell-hole this cycle of thoughts created was not something that I could easily talk about. The feelings would come up when I reached across our bed and touched the emptiness, or remembered the plans we had made to enjoy the rest of our lives. I lived and had my being anchored within the missing of something I believed I had lost and, in this process, lost myself to the pain.

I turned to some of the masterful teachers guiding my path, so that somehow I could reconcile myself to the loss of my joy partner. Now that all these years have passed, what I understand is that, in my dis-pair, and in the swirl of my deep emotional feelings of loss, I only perpetuated more feelings of loss. And actually, in doing this, for a time, I lost much of me.

Joy lost is a solitary journey. No one can enter that place with you, nor should they. No one can ever fill the void you experience, and you don't want them to. As I slowly search for every word right now, I want to be deliberate so that I can convey the sacredness with which I hold this joy of mine; the appreciation of the gifts of creativity, the love, and the blessing of Lee and my exquisite experience together with him. I appreciate, I am grateful, and I love life more than ever, which is something I know he would want for me. Joy is present in ways I never dreamed possible.

MY JOY PARTNER

Lee and I started our spiritual journey together when we moved from New York to Las Vegas. It was in Temple Ner Tamid that I really felt at home spiritually. I loved the sound of Hebrew words being chanted during prayers. I felt elated when I heard the Cantor sing the beautiful sacred music of the holidays. Being brought up Methodist in a small town in upstate New York, I was never exposed to different religions or people from different cultures. Because Lee was Jewish, I thought it would be a good experience for our family. And it was.

In 1984, we were introduced to Darryl Anka, who channeled Bashar. This group of beings was fresh and brought exciting information about the transformational life we are becoming aware of this day. Throughout the years, Lee and I participated in the sessions Bashar offered, causing a greater awareness that opened both of us to new ideas of our exciting future. I will always remember a communication when Bashar told us we were masters of limitation, that we had taken limitation to a degree no others in all the universes ever thought possible. We train ourselves to be limited through pain and suffering, thinking there is some reward waiting for us, but through the Law of Attraction, the reward is only more pain and suffering. Bashar told us that there are civilizations waiting to see how far humanity will go once we really understand the power of letting our resistance down.

Ironically, it was not until a few months ago, when I listened to the teachings of Abraham through Esther Hicks, that all the pieces of what both Seth and Bashar communicated really came into alignment for me.

Abraham-Hicks is teaching us something humans have all heard before; that we know on a soul-level, but in a new way we are now ready to hear. The teachings on the Law of Attraction are so completely opposite to the collective belief structures we have put in place that, at times, I feel like the slingshot of unlimited consciousness that Bashar described has just let go.

Earlier I wrote about the juxtaposition of excitement and loss in the same sentence. The teaching Abraham-Hicks has presented to us is with the clarity of a mountain lake. I thrill at seeing a waterfall spilling out of that lake and rushing past us as it finds its way into a greater ocean of delight and joy!

We are all eternal, vibrational beings living in a vibrational universe. Our physical expression is but a small portion of the greater source of who we are. Abraham calls It the Vortex of Creation, Seth described It as All That Is, and Bashar called It The Creator. They are all saying the same thing: because we are eternal beings, there is no death. When we have completed our original reason for coming here, we simply return to our own Vortex of Creation where All That Is resides.

There are civilizations waiting to see how far humanity will go once we really understand the power of letting our resistance down.

I finally understand the essence of the words of my long-time teacher and mentor Jesus, when He said, "I am in the world but not of it." This statement is my central theme for understanding the new paradigm in which we are now living.

I am in the world, but not of the world.

Filled With Light

I have grown more conscious and learned much through my experiences. Today I am not offended when someone chooses to take another road, or leaves this reality in whatever manner he or she chooses. When Lee left on his journey back into his vortex, and I was in the deepest despair I had ever felt, I could not stop crying. So I called Rita, a dear friend and psychotherapist. Sometimes I can "see" energies that reside in our auras. While talking with Rita, I stretched out on my lounge chair, pleading for some relief. As we talked, I began to see my own aura around my legs. What I saw in my aura looked like swiss cheese. My aura had holes and tears that I had never seen before. After sharing this with Rita, we hung up and I immediately went to my mentor Jesus to ask about what I was seeing.

Here is the gist of my conversation with Him. "When your partnership with another is very deep, when you have come to rely on him for certain things, when he fills many voids for you that you have allowed, there is a comingling of energies within your light bodies. And then, when there is an abrupt departure from this world, he assuredly takes his light body with him. Because death as such has not been fully understood until now, the grief feels devastating. Without understanding the process, you feel all those voids at once."

"So what do I do?" I asked.

"Fill the holes with your own light," He answered.

How many years of learning about codependency did it take for this realization to come to me? Life is really a spiraling of vibrational energies and we continue to ascend into greater and greater awareness of who we are and why we are.

To complete the story, that moment, I started to pull my own light from my greater self to fill those holes. I looked for areas where I depended on Lee and began to learn how to take care of those issues for myself. I was reaching beyond my self-imposed limitations and finding relief. Using the Goodness Process (see in Chapter 9) helped me bridge the false belief that I had done something wrong and because of that, Lee decided to leave. Declaring that I am the essence of pure goodness actually helped me to be closer to him and reexperience the wonderful life we shared. During this time, there were lots of tears and a pain in my heart that I thought would never leave. I learned how to see through my own brick walls, and I began to experience the other side of the wave of love in my life. Now, 10 years later, as I recall the experience and use my wisdom to help others who have lost a loved one, I so deeply appreciate our life together. I can tear up during a song we once adored, or when our family gathers on the holidays, but they are joyous tears. I have left the idea of the missing place behind by filling the holes within me. No longer lost in the devastation, I can truly say thank you with joy for this day. And in the words of my daughter Pam, "At the end of the day, I'm really glad I got to see the day."

I have always been able to communicate through the process of channeling with those who are non-physical. The Masters, such as Jesus, are easier for me because they have a deliberate focus to uplift mankind, and no agenda. However, on many occasions, I have also been able to bring through different personalities who have crossed over. The general purpose of these communications from the other side was to ease the pain of those who needed relief, including myself. I had felt Lee close to me for quite a long time after he entered his vortex; I knew his energy and how it felt.

While I was on my way to my grandson's school to pick him up one day, I began to hear…"In the Tomorrow of My Tomorrows" repeating over and over in my mind.

I knew a message was coming through and I hurried to write it down.

In the Tomorrow of My Tomorrows

AlixSandra Parness 2002
The voice of my husband Lee
(June 1930 – April 2001)

In the tomorrow of my tomorrows,
I will see you again.
I gaze upon your face
Filled with wisdom and joy.
Your eyes embrace my Being
And draw me close.
Across the galaxies I travel
And I find you just on the far
Side of my heart.
Through time and space I reach you,
Your song is sweet and pure.
I am filled now and complete.
I thank you my beloved,
For the gratitude in my heart is overflowing
As I bless our lives enfolded,
Caressed by millions of moments
We have before embraced.
You enriched me
And made me whole again.

MY REPLY

My Dearest Tender Soldier,
In the tomorrow of my tomorrows,
I shall once again
Know your gentle strength.
As you gather me in your arms
To laugh away the day.
There you are
Just across the way,
Standing in the window,
Watching me
Watching you,
Forever
in
the Light.

Actually, it was a few weeks after I received the poem when I realized that my dear, sweet, loving husband sent me this message. Tears flow even now as I remember the feelings of excitement that day as I read those words and *knew* they came from him. It was only then that my reply, through sobs of joy, came flowing from my heart. I had to include this particular poem because it is these powerful moments that teach us about our eternal nature and that joy is ever present, even when it feels as if our heart is breaking.

IDENTITY LOSS

Jeannie is a woman who had lost her identity in the lives of others. "I think I began to lose my identity a few years after I was married and became extremely ill with pelvic inflammatory disease that then robbed me of the ability to have children." Jeannie had loved the picture of herself she originally saw as a wife and mother—this was a dream she had had from the time she was a little girl. She wanted to have a husband who loved, adored, respected, and cherished her as she did him, and to have children to make their family complete. Wife and mother and teacher, that is who she said she wanted to be. This picture started to shatter and she didn't have the skills to rebuild a revised vision for her life. She knew that life was meant to be a happy experience, and wondered, how does happiness shatter? What goes wrong?

With a deep desire to be parents, Jeannie and her husband were blessed with two adopted children. It just so happened that both children had many emotional issues in their early developmental years, which led to challenges (more than most) in their teen and early adult years. Jeannie became their advocate and would find a way for them to navigate through this world, no matter what the cost to her.

When Jeannie first came to Inner Focus, she rarely left the house. She just waited for the activities of her husband and children to fill her day at home. While searching for help for one of her teenage children, she sought the help of an Inner Focus graduate and healer who helped her child, but more importantly, saw how lost Jeannie was and wanted to introduce her to our class. It would take 18 months before Jeannie could awaken, quite literally, to the powerhouse of a person sleeping inside her. "The Goodness Process words were so profound,"

Jeannie told me, "that I knew this was a turning point in starting to see the enormity of all that I am."

In the few short years that followed, we lost our dear friend and classmate Eleanor who had become Jeannie's mentor. The next year, Jeannie's mom died, and then suddenly her beloved husband also died. And through all of this chaos and loss, Jeannie began to discover and acquire the skills to unlock the power of who she was. She would come to know the joy that had always sustained her, and she was an advocate by example to her children as she began to see "the diamond in the rough" that her husband always said she was. Through her eyes, both children discovered the value of themselves and continue to see the essence in the goodness of their lives that has brought them through their personal issues and the death of their father, "their rock." The children are now both building happy and fulfilling lives nestled in the hammock of the journey Jeannie took to discover herself. *When she discovered her true joy,* her children began discovering the source of all that is inside of them. Now Jeannie and her children are each seeing that their lives are a gift to be lived in a state of joy.

Jeannie was determined to do all she could to show them a world of happiness and joy and love.

I asked Jeannie for help in telling about her journey for *Activate Joy*, and we finished this story together. Almost immediately, she received this note from her son. We were so thrilled that we just had to include it because it sang the confirmation of the shared journey to joy for Jeannie's family:

> "Mom, I need you to know and never doubt that I will always be okay. I'm not lost anymore, not quite to my "destiny," but I'm an adult who was lucky enough to have all four of my grandparents alive 'til my mid-20s and also having dad and you as truly

the best parents anyone could ever dream of. I feel blessed for this daily and for you teaching me the tools I need to live a happy life. So don't worry. I'm actually extremely motivated to achieve my dream! Love you."

I feel so privileged to know Jeannie and her family, and consider them friends. When Lee died, I didn't have all the tools then that I have now. It was so satisfying to share them with Jeannie when her husband passed. Our community gathered around Jeannie and the children to support and shelter them with all the love and uplifting of eternal friendship. In the process, Jeannie has discovered herself, she has become a true being of great power and light determined to live her life on the happy track. She shared something that was given to her during the Goodness Process healing… "Walk on the earth and fly with the angels, heaven and earth are the same."

You can do this, too. Letting go of doubt and grief is a major step. From there, regaining your power happens when you choose to believe in yourself, love who you are, just the way you are, and reach for more.

Joy is ever present even when our hearts are breaking.

Move on When You Are Ready

Like love, knowing comes from deep within your soul and cannot be disputed. If you have lost someone you love deeply, I encourage you to believe in yourself, believe in the love that surpasses all understanding, and realize that those who have completed their human journey are already jumping joyously as they embark on their new journey in non-physical form. I certainly realize the depth and breadth of the barrage of emotions from grief to anger to numbness that are at play for you, and it is my heartfelt intention to offer you some relief not only with my story, but with the various processes that you might be drawn to in this book.

I told Jeannie, "There will never be a time your love (her husband) will not be with you, and you must never try to 'get over it.' Instead, embrace your love, and when the tears come, allow the feelings, knowing they are like the waves of the ocean that ebb and flow. Practice diving through that wave until you can swim to the other side easily and with grace. It is in these moments the shift takes place and you can easily reactivate joy."

Sometimes well-meaning friends and family might say something such as, "It's been long enough, aren't you ready to move on?" Understand that advice is their pain speaking and not yours to follow. You will move on with your life as you ready yourself to do this because you just will—naturally. Life naturally calls us forward into a greater blessing and expansion when the pain of not following your own star is just too hard to bear. Later, your heart will fill with all the kind and joyous moments you shared as you celebrate *you* knowing your loved one is right there beside you cheering you on.

CHAPTER 4

UNIVERSAL LAWS

THE IMMUTABLE LAWS OF THE UNIVERSE ALWAYS
WORK ON OUR BEHALF.

A 3-year-old child can remind us just how easy it is to move from earth-shaking misery to laughter. Once I fell down and cut my leg so deeply it took several stitches to close the wound. After the screaming and crying came the relief of knowing I would be okay, and, after all, there was ice cream. All of us, regardless of age, know deep inside, on the most sacred personal level, that the purest feeling humans can experience is joy. Joy paves our way into more expansion with greater possibilities.

Immutable universal laws govern our existence here in this time-space reality. In our exploration of joy, I want you to be aware of two laws that, when understood and applied consciously, will make all the difference as you learn to allow your limitless life to unfold before you.

THE LAW OF ATTRACTION: WHAT GOES AROUND COMES AROUND

Our thoughts, our intentions, our deepest feelings are immediately granted. The Law of Attraction works like a boomerang. Send out worry, and you will receive more things to worry about. Stay in the grief of the missing place, and life will pass you by. Be a child who has lost all hope and feels he has a dark and unforgivable soul, and the Law of Attraction will be unwavering in bringing you experiences that underscore those beliefs. On the other hand, when you send out joy, joy is returned. This giant of a law is inclusive; it will leave no stone unturned, and never leaves anyone out. Attraction works like the circulatory system of our body. Blood gets pumped in and out from the heart and circulates in a closed system, like a mandala of great proportions. The job of this law is to give you what you want, whether it be good or bad, no matter what, without fail. *This law is neutral and only you direct the outcome.* The Law of Attraction is not new and it is not a secret. It consistently delivers back to you what you put out. The resonate frequency that you are vibrating in tune with draws to you experiences, items, and people of matching frequencies.

To expand this law a little further, we have to consider the fact that all we ever need do is align with what we want and allow it to be delivered to us. Today children are trained to expect and it is given to them. The "I" generation is living beyond the limitations you and I may have endured in this lifetime. They are the forerunners, our teachers, and our greatest assets. The promise that is within the pages of this book is that there is always another viewpoint, another side of the wave. You are never stuck, and you always have another chance to figure out how to live the life you really want.

The ramifications of this understanding reach far to remind us that we don't have to earn anything. The idea of hard work dissolves into activating the joy in our creative hearts, and through alignment with what we want, the Law of Attraction brings it to us. Imagine a world where this understanding is widespread...

THE LAW OF RESONANCE: YOUR THOUGHTS AND FEELINGS BRING THINGS TO YOU

This law is very important because the Law of Attraction relies on the *resonance* of your thoughts and feelings to bring things to you. Resonance is an energy field that calls forth similar frequencies without discrimination, negative or positive.

It is the frequency or tonal quality of our thoughts and emotions that activates the Law of Resonance. Whatever you think, repeated over and over again with increased feeling, will set up the matching frequencies, or resonance. The Law of Attraction *uses* those frequencies activated by resonance to bring you a matching experience. The Law of Resonance is impersonal and works consistently through your expectations and heightened state of the way you *feel* about what you are expecting. You may think that the Law of Attraction and The Law of Resonance are the same, but each has a different intention. For example, in 1984, I named my school Inner Focus for no other reason than it sounded good. However, throughout the years, I came to understand the resonate frequency of those two words: inner focus. In repeating that name over and over, it became sacred. The concept of inner focus became reinforced. The vibration of those words created a vortex of joy and wisdom where people were drawn to learn more about themselves and their own inner focus.

Here is the key: Whatever you think, repeated with feelings, will set up a matching resonate frequency. The Law of Attraction *uses* that frequency to bring you what you have asked for. The Law of Resonance is impersonal and works consistently all the time through your expectations and heightened state of the way you *feel* about what you are expecting.

Inner focus calls joy into being because the resonate frequency of your focus is centered on *you*. Almost everyone who has come to study with me has the same goals. They want to discover themselves, heal themselves, and learn to be happy. In order to do that, they must focus within themselves and learn to value themselves and their feelings first and foremost.

INNER FOCUS, OUTER CREATION

Through unconscious use of these two laws, without realizing the implications, we have been trained away from the natural joy with which we came into this world. We have trained ourselves into questioning our value, and our worthiness, to the nth degree. I have worked with people who are convinced they don't have a right to exist, that the world would be better off without them. Through understanding these two laws, using deliberate intention to create the reality they would prefer to be living, a change of consciousness is assured. With just a little practice, they create their preferred and happier reality.

Your belief system will show you precisely how you think, both positively and negatively:

> *It's hard.*
>
> *That's easy.*
>
> *It's fun.*
>
> *It's such a burden.*
>
> *I'd get in trouble.*
>
> *Gosh, I could never…*

How you *think* and what you *believe* to be true creates a resonate frequency that activates the Law of Attraction.

The Law of Attraction is immutable and will *always* give you what you want, every time, without fail, whether you are aware of its power or not. What is happening in your relationships with people, and with money and health, are excellent barometers for you to watch to become more aware of what you are asking to attract.

I was introduced to the Abraham-Hicks teachings on the Law of Attraction in April 2010. Attending a one-day class in Albuquerque, sitting in the front row, I listened to a very familiar voice. Stunned at the familiar phrases and use of ideas, I was on cloud nine. Abraham was talking about ideas and concepts I had been using in my work for years. They gave a name to the process I had naturally accessed many years ago, sitting with Jane Roberts listening to her channel Seth as they wrote the book, *The Nature of Personal Reality.*

Learning about what Abraham calls the Vortex of Creation gave me a more refined understanding of how we create our reality, showing us how to speak with deliberate, positive intention and bask and allow happiness to be the operative word of the day, opening my creative floodgates. I have been so blessed in my life, and I treasure each milestone along the way. I so deeply appreciate all of my mentors and teachers, seen and unseen. Abraham, channeled through Esther Hicks, feels to me like a profoundly unifying force. Jesus said, "Let those who have ears to hear, hear this." I for one hear you, Abraham, and bless the days to come.

What are you attracting? Is it more to be joyful about or things that burden you? This chapter is just a small glimpse into the Laws of Attraction and Resonance. You will read many mentions of the Law of Attraction throughout this book and easily learn how to live your life beyond limitations and become the joyful deliberate creator you were born to be.

CHAPTER 5

GETTING TO KNOW YOUR YABBITS

CONTRARY THOUGHTS, OPINIONS, AND IDEAS
WILL SPLIT US OFF FROM THE PURE FREQUENCY OF
ACCEPTANCE AND LOVE THAT CAME WITH US INTO THIS
EXPERIENCE.

I gave a talk at my church one Sunday morning on the Art of Positive Thinking. Usually I have an outline to keep me centered, however, this particular morning, I remember being aggravated about the "stuff" that seems to pop up when we are doing our best to stay positive. I remember getting off the track of joy onto a series of the "yah-buts" in my head. When those yah-buts happen to me, I sit up and take notice. I know I hit on something important because it's like a slap on the head saying, "Slow down and pay attention." Now, I had the seed ideas forming for my talk. The rest was easy. It happens to everyone...as soon as you try to stay in a positive attitude about something, it seems as if every excuse in the world surfaces to bring you out of that happy place. The whole thing was very humorous. As I flowed with the talk and explained the yah-buts to everyone, it was received with joyous applause.

I became excited with the results that emerged from that morning's talk; I was inspired and wanted to expand the idea further. The next weekend, I invited some friends to join me at the church. I brought my sewing machine and materials, such as fabrics, buttons, threads, and adornments. As we talked about what I was beginning to call our "Yabbits," we made little free-form Yabbit dolls to represent whatever negative voice might be coming up. Actually, I used those little darlings for years as examples of negative thoughts: *Yah-but I can't do that, Yah-but I'm not as creative as you are.* People loved them because in the pain of the moment, the Yabbit dolls would make them smile. Somehow transformation is so much easier when joy is present.

What Is a Yabbit?

Because I use the term *Yabbit* throughout this book, let's see what it really means.

You already know the Yabbits; they are the voices inside your head, the doubts and the put-downs in your mind. "After all," the Yabbits say, "look at all the bad things you've done! Don't have a job yet? I'm not surprised." The Yabbits can easily convince you that you're not as good as you would like to believe you are. "No one wants to hear what you have to say. Don't bother with your dream because it won't come true. Anything you want to say or do has already been done, and much better than you could do it." We have the Yabbits about other people. Usually these Yabbits reinforce the idea that others are not really as well put together as you. There will be lots more about these guys a few pages from now.

Does any of this sound remarkably familiar?

Yabbits are the voices that argue against you.

Our Yabbits were programmed early in life and were originally designed to keep us safe. Yabbits have helped us stay safe by keeping us in line, and they are responsible for helping to manage our physical well-being. *Yah that looks like fun, but you better not do that or else you'll break your arm. Yah-but if anyone*

finds out, you'll get in a heap of trouble. Yah-but you don't know how to drive yet. So sometimes the yah-buts really do keep us safe, but as time passes, things change.

Yabbits are sub-personalities

In traditional therapies, my version of the Yabbits might be called sub-personalities. The personality you have today has evolved since birth, and throughout the years grew to be made up of several sub-personalities. Each sub-personality or Yabbit develops distinct voices, along with overtones of different voices that have evolved since our birth. Even though the voices are powerful and persuasive, there is only one core you, and that "you" is a worthy, deserving person with the wherewithal to be and do anything you can conceive. More than that, you are a vibrational being in a state of constantly becoming all that you want and desire.

Contrary thoughts, opinions, and ideas will split us off from the purity of the frequency we came here with, creating a static environment that does not move. What we call sub-personalities hold this pattern for us, until we are ready to change it. Each sub-personality is a vibrational pattern of energy that interrupts the frequency of our True Being—our Source Self.

The sub-personality energy pattern present in any given moment seems to operate independently of the True Self. When you follow the directions of the sub-personalities, it leaves a bad taste in your mouth. This is the feeling you want to pay attention to the most. Focus on this feeling and it will show you what you do not want. Once you realize that your thoughts are keeping you in a place you do not like, make a deliberate choice to shift into alignment with what you really want by giving what you want the focus of your attention.

How are the sub-personalities formed?

Sub-personalities are literally formed when our needs are not met—to be loved, to belong, to feel safe and secure, and to be fed, are the major needs. There is an automatic fail-safe mechanism within the human psyche that launches a champion that comes to the rescue. When we perceive this energy as real and then come to rely on it over and over again, a sub-personality is formed.

Let's look at Joanne's sub-personality of the *pleaser*. In order to get her needs met, Joanne learns that she can get her needs met when she is agreeable, hiding her true feelings, which may be different from the ones she has just given in to. In doing this, she feels safe. Throughout life, especially as she is growing up, Joanne is rewarded for agreeable behavior patterns, and punished for being rebellious. Whenever she gets attention through the reinforcement of "good girl" comments, she might want to continue on that path rather than risk feeling her own feelings, and thinking her own thoughts. In other words, sub-personalities can become energetically "stuck," as the Yabbits continually remind her that being stuck is good and safe. Joanne is being served by feeling loved, and getting the positive attention of those she sees as authority figures in her life through negative self-esteem. However, the price paid is to continue to hide the joy identity that she knew as a child—keeping her True Self safely tucked away, hidden behind painful codependent patterns.

Can you see how sub-personalities become the Yabbits that often dominate our life? By allowing us the false perception of control over our environment, protecting our vulnerability, and exerting power over others, many times we give the Yabbits top-billing in our lives. Throughout the years, these patterns grow stronger and more certain of their influence. As with anything you focus on, every time you listen to the negative whispers and follow the trail the Yabbits leave, their thought patterns become stronger and stronger. Through this evolution, they will implement their own agendas without regard to the wants and desires of your True Self. The purpose served is negative self-esteem, which I explain later in the book.

Without deliberately choosing our thought patterns, the Yabbits can rise to become a force that undermines confidence and snuffs out the creative flame. When we become "attached," it is like hanging onto the submerged anchor of a boat with the engine running. By refusing to let the boat go on its way, the engine overheats, and eventually quits running; the boat rots and begins to sink, and the sharks (Yabbits) circle the carnage. And those Yabbits of others and ourselves will tear us to bits if we let them. For example, there is always a Yabbit behind the fear of allowing our magnificence to shine. Yabbits make rules to follow and then stand with their arms crossed if we should stray too far outside the lines.

YABBITS PROVIDE GROWTH OPPORTUNITIES

On the other side of this, each sub-personality also has a positive intention. Hidden in the core of its energy is the elusive *joy*. Hope is always present. Ultimately, each Yabbit provides an opportunity to grow. We are guided by our Soul, bringing experience that moves us into conscious awareness, balance, alignment, and integration. My intention as a pastor or a teacher is to inspire and offer new ideas for my audience to consider and perhaps become inspired by. As I prepared for my talk on "The Art of Positive Thinking" and Yabbits yabbitted in my ear trying to distract me, I understood the purpose of their actions. I became amused and creatively decided to use the event as a teaching. The result was to get many people involved in a craft project making these little stuffed dolls, and then having them on a shelf in my lectern to toss into the audience or use humorously to bring home a point. Knowledge is the key here; understanding that there is nothing out to harm you no matter what it may look like, then using your wisdom to reveal the true intent and bring out the joy.

Without deliberately choosing our thought patterns, the Yabbits can rise to become a force that undermines confidence and snuffs out the creative flame. When we become "attached," it is like hanging onto the submerged anchor of a boat with the engine running.

The following is a brief list of some of the more influential Yabbits in our lives. Using the skills of intention and conscious awareness, read through the list slowly and allow the tone of each Yabbit to show itself to you. I have intentionally used spare definitions for you to make your own natural associations. Notice the pitch of each voice, the tenor and the depth of influence in your life.

MOST INFLUENTIAL YABBITS

- **Judge Yabbit** with his jury of hangmen
- **Parental Yabbit** controlling her family
- **Jealous Yabbit** and his committee of comparisons
- **Nagging Bossy Yabbit** with her entourage of perfectionist thugs
- **Pleaser Yabbit** giving in to everyone else's ideas
- **Righteous Yabbit** with her congregation of certainties
- **Moral Yabbit** and her ogres of rationalization
- **Doom and Gloom Yabbits** with daily reports on Chicken Little's falling skies
- **Shadow Yabbit** with his cloaking devices and league of tempters and seducers
- **Wounded Yabbit** with her incessant crying that opens her wound over and over
- **Lonely Yabbit** and her debilitating companions of sadness
- **Hoarding Yabbit** with his compulsive board of directors
- **Let's Wait and See Yabbit** with her never-ending waiting room filled with postponers, procrastinators, and never-get-it-done-rs

Entrainment

During a lifetime, we become used to the Yabbits' melodies and overtones that weave into the tapestry of our thoughts and belief systems. Many of us are entrained to the Yabbits that make us feel less, thinking that's the way we "should" feel. Forgetting our worthiness and inherent goodness, Yabbits of negative self-esteem force us to look elsewhere for guidance, and often, when we follow the ideas of others, we become dissatisfied, discouraged, disgruntled, and unhappy. We can become buried underneath so many "shoulds" and "should nots" that we completely lose who we are. Some people are so entrenched in negative self-esteem, they seem to disown themselves. The hopelessness therein can become so profound that the trail it often leads to is suicide in one form or another. When we lose our guidance system that tells us we are a worthy, deserving person, we've temporarily lost the joy that brought us here to begin with.

Hoarding Yabbits

I watched a popular television program—so popular that there are hours of this particular subject devoted to our daytime and prime-time screen: *Hoarders*. "Are you a hoarder?" a counselor to the hoarders asks. "No, I'm not a hoarder, I'm a collector," they say emphatically. As I watched several of these stories, I could see the Yabbit theme present in their lives. So attached to their garbage, one woman had to compulsively go through her trash several times before she could let an empty tuna can go. If this TV show is a valuable commodity to the networks and news media, we have to ask why. What is the higher message in the reawakening process that wants our attention?

Because every action always has a positive intention behind it, the positive force on the opposite side of the negative force of hoarding is deliberate choice. To deliberately choose is a selective process, and through intention it naturally employs positive self-esteem. To hoard is an obsessive process done through negative self-esteem.

Hoarding creates suffering, and another sparkle in the kaleidoscope of negative thinking. Suffering can become a compulsive action run entirely by a committee of Yabbits telling you that you will feel better doing the same thing over and over again, traveling down the same path constantly while seemingly staying safe. When we continually allow this behavior in our lives, we so identify with it that it becomes our imprisoned reality. Sifting through garbage becomes an everyday activity, holding your breath, tensing your muscles, closing your eyes because the tightness is so overwhelming, and yet, with time, it really seems normal. Allowing this behavior as a constant activity without relief slowly turns off the "pilot light," desensitizing us to the cries of our loved ones, and ultimately to the screams within that want to be released.

The hoarding shows are sending a message to our collective subconscious, shaking us out of the Yabbit slumber. Wake up! Take control of your thoughts and let yourself feel joy. Stop defending your position. Come out of isolation and see the beauty of the world you chose to live in. Allow yourself to love and to be loved.

Yabbits show us what we don't want, what not to do.

In every case I have seen, there is always a family member or friend who intervenes because, from their vantage point, the Hoarding Yabbit world has cut them off from someone they love. Reaching out to close the gap—the abyss of isolation—is the hand of love and concern. You can see the impact on their faces and in their voices. One daughter says, "I'm the trash; my mother won't throw her garbage away, she threw me away instead."

Hoarding your affections is extreme impoverishment, the level of separation is profound, the tears heart-wrenching. There is mounting debt that becomes physically evident. There is profound scarcity of freedom, of space, no place to rest, no peace. These are extreme cases; we can clearly see the impact of the Yabbit world on everyone involved. The levels of despair (separation) for all concerned shake the cocktail of thinking and thought processes, beliefs, and certainties. If we keep drinking this same cocktail, we cannot effectively choose and allow the joy-filled reality we really want into our experience.

We are all looking for the joy in our lives. The Yabbits are way-pointers. They are there to show us what we don't want, what not to do. They jump up and down until they get our attention, even under piles of garbage thinking.

Now look at your Yabbit hoarders. We all have our little piles of garbage we refuse to let go of. Even as you read these words, your Yabbit committee is bringing out the lists for you to look at, and go over once again. They do that because it is their job. Every time you bring up old patterns of thought, there is a new opportunity to make a different choice. You are the only one who can close the gap from despair to happiness. And as you become more and more aware of this truth, resolve to be a deliberate creator of your own reality. Resolve to make more conscious choices, hushing the Yabbits, quelling their chants.

Shadow Yabbit

The shadow begins by using Yabbit doubts to undermine the emerging tender light of our creative genius, casting clouds of confusion that shield the Light from you. The Light says, "Believe in yourself, you know the truth." The Shadow Yabbit says, "It's never worked before and it won't work now." This is bunk. We can often hold our light in this situation. So the Shadow Yabbit might decide to make a stronger case, tempting you further.

Sometimes the shadow puffs itself up, and works through people in a group to devalue and destroy individuals or perhaps a whole group structure itself. We have seen this happen time after time in many groups, and recently in the group consciousness of the government of the American people. The shadow strives to splinter groups and even personalities for its purpose of separation. Here is the positive intent: splintering and separating so that you can be empowered to say no! That is not what I want and I refuse to give it any thought, I refuse to follow those people, I refuse to entertain that belief system. I think my own thoughts and feel my own feelings, thank you very much.

Have you ever noticed how the devaluing energy escalates as the truth becomes more and more clouded? The shadow wants you to think you are not strong enough to hold your Light, and therefore you are not ready for the next step. The shadow invites other Yabbit energies to see how far they can push you before you say *enough*.

In essence, rising above the Yabbits' chatter is an initiation or an emergence into a new level of awareness, and this is a process. We experience it collectively and on individual levels. What is relevant about initiation here is recognizing a greater truth than one you have previously known, and then living from that truth.

The chatter from the Shadow Yabbits is seductive. Know that the Shadow Yabbits are really like hired stage hands. Stage hands do not write the script; you are the writer of your own life. You get to choose the players and how your life will unfold. Know that this was meant to be great fun and joyful. So what is it that goes wrong? When we begin to believe the story the Yabbits tell us and attach to the pain and suffering, we live *from* rather than *beyond* limitation.

Well, that time is ending. The truth is that right now the power of the Yabbit world is receding, taking away the curtain forever and playing life out in the round so everyone can see all sides of the players.

Taming Your Yabbits

Reflection: Take time to reflect on how many times the Yabbit world has affected your life. What part did you play? What were the results? In the end, where did you end up?

The process of spiritual maturing uses the Yabbits as transformational tools to dismantle old ideas and worn-out belief systems.

Spiritual maturity develops through conscious awareness and self-reflection by choosing the ease and flow of happiness rather than putting up with pain and suffering. Spiritual maturity develops as we empower ourselves to expand with life. Now that you have knowledge of the Yabbit world and some idea of how they operate in your life, let's turn the tables and learn to use them as transformational tools. I suggest getting a notebook you can use to journal your revelations.

Begin by looking over the list of Yabbits and picking one or two that really jump off the page. Remember they are really your friends that you have programmed to keep you safe. Just begin to write about how this Yabbit is affecting your life and your happiness. Perhaps that other Yabbit over there has gotten out of control and forgotten that you are still the captain of your own ship. Talk about the need to take back your own power and make your own conscious decisions. During the process, joy will knock on your door and will surely bring you messages of hope. The further you go to allow your joy-based expectations to sweep you along into the arms of happiness, hope will show up to shine the way, aligning you with the power of your heart's desire.

Stop! Open the door and begin to write those messages in your journal. Make those thoughts relevant in your day. Focus on joy and allow the Law of Attraction to bring you what you really want.

Spiritual maturity is *knowing*.

Here is that stairway to heaven:

- **Tell the truth** to yourself as best you can about the thoughts you are cycling through repeatedly.

- **Be self-reflective.** Monitor your emotional guidance system. Follow the path of ease and flow, feeling good about yourself at all times.

- **Decide to be a selective thinker.** Thank the Yabbit committee for taking such good care of your trash-thoughts; these are the beliefs that make you feel awful, but you keep on thinking them, hoping you will feel better for thinking them.

- **Select the thoughts that make you feel good;** gather and keep thinking those thoughts. Become joyful.

- **Dissolve negative thoughts** that make you feel ashamed, less than, or bad about yourself in any way. Light dissolves the dark. When you walk into a dark room and turn the light on, the darkness does not argue with you, it simply dissolves in the joy of light.

Stay with me as we continue to turn the kaleidoscope of joy that will help get your naturally joyous nature in high gear.

CHAPTER 6

FROM THE PAIN OF CONFORMING, TO JOY

THE PAIN OF CONFORMITY IS TRANSMUTED INTO THE
JOY OF DELIBERATELY CREATING THE REALITY YOU
PREFER. CHALLENGES BECOME ADVENTURES. LAUGHTER
REPLACES ANGER. EVERYTHING GOES YOUR WAY, ALL
THE TIME.

I once watched the movie *Pleasantville.* If you remember this movie, it was the story of a town stuck in a black-and-white setting with residents who didn't want change. The inhabitants of Pleasantville had no idea that a world beyond their immediate town even existed. They had never seen anything—a flower, a bird, a painting, or themselves—in color. The roads led nowhere. It seemed that circling around and around would keep things pleasant, so everyone just agreed to that idea without question or doubt. Then Bud, a hero in the story, showed up with his sister from another time-space reality. Bud and his sister brought their light bodies and conscious awareness of the expanded universe they knew about and lived in. They brought their experiences, knowledge of color, and more, which impacted the vibrational frequencies of the town.

As the movie told the story of the awakening of the people of Pleasantville, I couldn't help but realize the parallels to our story today. Factions of our human family are steeped in tradition handed down for generations. Some of those traditions involve long-held ideas of morality, the rules of engagement, deeply held resentments, resistance to embracing differences, and deep-seated hatred for cultures, people, or lifestyles unlike their own. These resistant ideas hold back our power. Most organizations teach conformity and separation, rather than encouraging the uniqueness of your own creative nature and union with the whole human family.

Conforming is painful. Conformity goes against our creative spirit and natural curiosity. Conformity dulls our senses, creating a society of automatons. Conformity is challenged, all day, every day, by people who demand their right to be themselves, to think their own thoughts and feel their own feelings without being judged.

Imagine a world where we embrace the differences we see every day, happily, joyously, with a deep and abiding interest. A world where everyone has whatever they want whenever they want it. Places we can sit back, and marvel at the creativity of the human spirit. Parents who trust their children completely to do whatever they want to do to explore their creative nature.

BEING A CONSCIOUS DELIBERATE CREATOR

Throughout my lifelong journey, I would have to say the previous statement brings me to the heart of my life purpose, and I believe yours as well. I remember the day a friend of mine gave me the book *Seth Speaks* and I stayed up all night devouring every word. Looking back on that night, I was more than hopeful about my life; I felt like I had been given the greatest gift anyone could ever receive. You see, I was the consummate pleaser. Growing up in a home that seemed loving and perfect from the outside but was often very different behind closed doors, you learn to do what you can to survive. Being a pleaser and being forced to conform to what others believe and want for you is a spirit-breaker for some. For me, I lived two lives: one at home and one outside. As a young woman, I never could reconcile the two until that night. The words "you create your own reality" resonated so deep within me, they broke my shackles. The next morning, as I told my husband all about my revelations, I realized the paradigm shift that had just occurred in my life. I was so aligned with the truth of my being; I was on a natural high for several years.

The next step was the letting go of the long-held hurts and certainties that closed me off from my greater self. This healing for me happened when I discovered Werner Erhard of the Human Potential Movement and Erhard Seminars Training (EST).

Through their grueling regimen of truth-telling, I was finally able to realize my own power, and from there, grew and flourished, deliberately creating and carving out my life according to my desires and needs. I changed so radically during those years that my family just stood back awestruck.

Joy Power
Tell the Truth.
Realize Your Power.
Be Deliberate.

Once I crossed the bridge into self-power, I looked back to see what path had led me to this apex. In essence, I discovered that I had crossed over three very specific bridges, and with each one I experienced an epiphany that opened up new worlds of joy.

First Bridge: Awareness

With the first bridge comes deep awareness that you alone create your own reality.

That statement sums up the truth of being in this human existence, that an idea creates a sympathetic vibration, which in turn creates a resonate frequency that aligns you with the source of you, immediately calling the Law of Attraction into action. Most is done by default without the awareness that you are indeed creating each and every step. You see you are the only uncooperative component to aligning with what you really want. You alone have control to live life the way you want to and not according to the direction of another. After all, to admit that means you have become self-responsible and take responsibility for all your life and all the choices that have been made along the way.

Second Bridge: Gathering

With the second bridge, you often grope around to figure out how to create your own reality.

EST created an atmosphere that broke down my defenses, which was really needed at that time. Whether you adopt the defense of a pleaser, or rebel, or anything in between to conform to what others want from you, you have to create layer upon layer of reasons not to be your true and authentic self. Werner was a leading-edge teacher then and helped people learn how, through their own self-revelations, to live happier and more productive lives. It sure worked for me. So the second bridge is gathering tools that work for you and then working them until you find the ones that are consistent with creating what you really want.

Now I want to introduce a term from the Abraham-Hicks teachings that I just love: cooperative components. You have heard it said that when the student is ready, the teacher appears, and I am sure you have experience in realizing that statement as fact in your life. Can't we all point to many instances when we are in just the right place at the right time? Or, someone might suggest something to you, and several months or years later, that seed ripens and is in alignment for the birthing of that idea.

Cooperative components are all the people and situations we draw to us to help us expand into a greater realization of who we are. When we look at our life from this perspective, things feel quite different. There is empowerment here. There is deliberate choice. There is fun and adventure awaiting…

Third Bridge: Implementing

With the third bridge, as a conscious deliberate creator, you implement those tools.

Up until this bridge, perhaps there isn't much in the way of deliberate creating.

Listen

We have been trained into the limitation of conforming. To move beyond limitations means that we joyfully "cross the bridge" to become a deliberate creator.

In the decades of my experience teaching, healing, and helping people discover their true selves, this idea of self-responsibility is the single-most difficult one to bridge, but once you see the value and implement the tools you have gathered, the empowerment that follows is exhilarating. You will then discover another great truth that may be hard to understand. This truth is that everyone else's reality is irrelevant to yours. You are now and always have been the most important person in your life.

There are no right tools to find and there are no wrong tools, either. No matter how you proceed, you will be okay and everything will work out for you. Maybe now is the right time for you to sit in the driver's seat and choose to make your own choices deliberately. I know it certainly is for me, and the joy that is activating every day is ecstatic.

Crossing this third bridge is an exhilarating phase of our journey together. In the early 1990s, I was teaching about the dismantling of codependency, another form of conformity. with ideas such as, "I can't be happy without you," or "I can only thrive if I give everything away," or "Be good and make me proud; you know everything you do is a reflection on your mother and me,"—now that was the trip I lived with. In codependency, you disappear. Your sole reason to live is to make someone else happy so you can be happy. There *is* no you.

The Yabbit you will encounter along this bridge says, "What about them?" People who begin this conscious journey need to have the question answered, "What about them?" How do they figure in? Isn't their reality part of my reality? So here it is—I finally have the answer to this question.

Everyone in your life is a cooperative component that shows up
to help you focus on your joy,
on what will make you happy,
on fulfilling your desires
and creative intentions.

The pain of conformity is transmuted into the joy of deliberately creating the reality you prefer. Challenges become adventures. The blame game turns into "Look what I just did!" Laughter replaces anger. Everything goes your way, and it seems like it happens all the time. The world becomes an exciting exploration, kind of like it was when you first came here. Only now you are grown and in charge of your own life, and you never need to conform to what anyone else wants of you again. Now deliberate choice is the order of the day.

CHAPTER 7

HOW DO I GET THERE? BASKING INTO ALIGNMENT

TO SHIFT GEARS, I REACH INTO MY MEMORY BANK THAT IS FILLED WITH MILLIONS OF POSITIVE MEMORIES, AND DELIBERATELY CHOOSE TO FEEL GOOD.

For a moment, I reach back in time, sifting through my memories to activate the happy times I knew as a child. I take all the precious time that I need to vividly recall these feelings, and the loving thoughts that make me feel good all over again. Basking is allowing those warm and soothing sensations or feelings to wash over me for as long as I can allow it. Basking washes away my troubles, bringing me into alignment with the powerful and uplifting energy of joy.

Children live in the moment. They take any opportunity to express their joy, even finger painting with spaghetti on walls. After all, that wall is a pretty big canvas with no limitations for a little one's vast imagination. I appreciate those memories and I want to remember more of them.

Sometimes when I am processing something difficult, perhaps a challenge that is always in my face, no matter how hard I try to free myself, it won't go away. When I experience something in which there seems to be no joy at all, that's when I shift gears and bask, softening my way. Lighting up and stumbling along the dark path of condemnation, making my way through the thickets of brambles and thorns, I step gently across the sharp stones until, there at the edge of the trees, beams of sunshine float toward me.

To shift gears, I reach into my memory bank that is filled with millions of positive memories, and deliberately choose to feel good. I notice the details, such as the sight and smell of wildflowers growing in damp ground. In silent thought, I reach for the warmth of the sun and then let go. To bask, bring forth the crowds of joyous moments woven into the fabric of your life. Sit down on a log and rest, feel relief and the expansion of joy aligning the myriad of thoughts and emotions flowing, flowing, flowing...

Happy thoughts are powerful because they have already been activated.

THE BASKING PRACTICE

1. **Allow thoughts to awaken within you those moments that bring smiles.** Reach for happy thoughts that want to bubble up to the surface. These happy reflections are powerful because they have already been activated. The joy inside you might have been tickled as it resonated with the memories that I shared. Other people's stories can reach out to you to activate your joy.

2. **Now, allow your joy to release your own happy thoughts,** those thoughts that every child shares, and that your inner child and mine just shared.

3. **Don't overwork the process,** just allow yourself to naturally open up.

4. **Maintain gentle focus on happy thoughts.**

5. **Acknowledge unhappy thoughts.** Acknowledge it and just keep moving deeper into your own personal joy. Allow joy the supreme moment in your reverie without getting distracted.

6. **Find one thought that really gives you a reason to stop, take notice, and laugh.** Talk to yourself about every little second of that experience you can recall. Use feeling words that open your heart.

Basking Example

I just love the feeling of the warm sun on my back. What fun it was to run down the street smelling the flowers that grew everywhere. It felt so good to know the flowers were all there waiting for me to come by and say hello each day. When it rained, I tromped through puddles on my way to find flowers for my mom, and, well, that was the best moment. I loved it when I brought a handful of tulips to Mommy. It felt as if the flowers made everyone happy. Mom always looked at me a little funny when she asked, "Now where did you get these?" And I bubbled, "Marion's of course; she wants you to be happy." I will always feel good when I see tulips. I just love tulips; I don't know why; I just do...

Basking allows me to not focus on the bad experiences from my childhood. I know people are used to hearing people focus on only the trauma of abused children. Although some of my childhood was violent, it does not mean that I wouldn't feel good bringing flowers to my mother and that she would not enjoy the experience, too. Actually, I am proud of the fact that I am able to not focus on the pain and feel the joy instead!

BASKING BEYOND BETRAYAL

My friend Ron was having a difficult time dealing with his brother. Money was at the heart of his pain. Ron and his brother had entered into an agreement years ago regarding an inheritance. However, his brother changed the agreement without telling Ron, and when Ron confronted him, his brother could see no problem with his decision. Ron had given away his power and his anger smoldered over time. When he and I talked about it, I could see that he was completely in a quagmire.

I offered the basking practice to assist him. He loved it and has continued to use the following as something to give him some relief from the circulating negative thoughts.

Basking Example

Life is good. I love my life. I get to do the things I want to do and I get to feel good most of the time. Every now and then feelings come up around feeling betrayed. When that happens, I really don't feel so good and life seems to slow down.

Today I am making a new decision. When I get triggered into thoughts of betrayal, I stop and take a moment to visit the "nothing" box. I recognize that old patterns are irrelevant to my feeling good now! All that matters in this moment is to come into balance with my good nature and myself. I know everything always works out for me. I know my life is abundant and filled with all good things. I love the feeling of being on a golf course with my buddies. I love the joy of the open air and the stretches of abundant green grass in front of me. I love the excitement of meeting new people and experiencing new and wonderful things each time it happens. It seems silly from this vantage point to hold on to old hurts; they are really irrelevant to where I am today.

Instead, I can bless the situations and the people involved. I see how I have grown and expanded in my heart and I want to expand even more. I stand in the center of my true and authentic self and I am glad. The air smells fresher. I have a clear vision of myself free and easy with life. I love life. I love myself and I appreciate all that occurs in my life because "It's all good."

DO THAT WHICH BRINGS YOU JOY
RIGHT NOW

As you continue reading, you will notice an energetic transmission that I have deliberately encoded within the stories and ideas that I am sharing with you. Years of teaching and healing allow me access to a blueprint, a matrix of delicious proportions designed to activate joy in everyday life.

Here is a basking statement that I am using right now. It really helps brings me into joy whenever I say it, and it works well with people who are experiencing loss and grief:

I declare that in my life there is no loss, there is only forward movement. My vision is clear as I look into my world with anticipation. All the experiences that have brought me to this place I bless, honor, and appreciate. Now my vista is wide open and I hold no one responsible for my happiness but me. The Source of me is dedicated to loving me unconditionally and allowing me the freedom to soar like an eagle.

Alignment with joy is imperative to living the life we came here to live. Joy is our birthright.

Well-meaning parents and cultures have trained the joy out of most of us. The day will come when we will be drawn spontaneously into the joyous activities of our children. What fun it would have been to join in the wall-painting experience that night just to see where those two children would have taken it. The day is dawning when the creative genius within joy will be revered instead of taking second place to competition and accomplishments. Striving for perceived success and money so often becomes our focus as we try to compensate for the lack of the true joy that allows us to thrive in our daily experiences.

There is a "fortune" awaiting everyone. Beyond the idea of money it is "for–tuning" up, getting ready to allow unlimited joy right now, beginning to allow joy into your life in a powerful way. You can bask by simply watching the wind softly move the leaves on that tree over there, or being delighted when a squirrel runs down a branch and noticing the movement of the bark under its tiny feet. Feel the rays of the sun as they peek through, warming your cheeks. Living in joy is living freely in the moment, allowing that mighty vortex of joy to call you in.

Basking is a powerful tool for shifting gears from the thoughts you no longer wish to focus on to recognizing the greater picture that you have already begun to paint. Your life is your canvas, brand new and blank every day. Get ready for the positive path of joy to open for you.

You Create Your Own Reality

How Thoughts and Emotions Create Reality

Inspiration from within.

Thoughts and ideas are attracted to the inspiration.

Emotion gathers around the thoughts and ideas.

Your reality is created from your thought forms
fueled by your emotions around the idea.

Remember

Emotion indicates the resonate frequency of the idea.

Emotion is the indicator of direction
toward what you want.

The thought pattern is the vibrational frequency
that causes the reality to manifest.

Excitement is the key to your future!

CHAPTER 8

THE ART OF BLESSING

WHEN ONE RECOGNIZES A BLESSING IS WITHIN THEM, THAT GIFT IS AUTOMATICALLY PRESENT FOR OTHERS TO EXPERIENCE.

Because the vibrations of my experiences still exist within me, expanded, embodied, and enlivened through my living of them, that same vibrational blessing is transmitted through the words you just read. Take a breath and feel it; call the blessings forward into your day. When one recognizes a blessing is within each thought, word, and deed, that gift is automatically present for others to experience.

We bless or condemn, often automatically without really thinking about it. If we like something, we give it our blessing, and if we don't, we join the chorus of Yabbits and often ruthlessly condemn.

Can you feel the buildup of energy leading to the awakening of your true power?

Developing the art of blessing is perhaps the easiest of all because blessing is a part of the very fabric of our being.

Do you realize that, by condemning others, we simply keep ourselves from expanding into the greatest life we could ever know? The life every one of us has envisioned and dreamed of can and does exist. In essence, to condemn is to contract, virtually cutting yourself off from access to your hopeful vision for the future and the promise that your dreams will manifest in your lifetime.

Here is how it works: when you think a thought, that thought creates a vibration that can be heard; it becomes a song or a frequency that is transmitted throughout your "light body," which is emitted from within your aura. No matter what song you sing, you are a blessing, and you are of great value to the world. Perhaps the time has come for you and I to make a new choice, to deliberately create the world we prefer to live in and not settle for what the Yabbits in the media world of mass consciousness tell us.

To be a deliberate creator requires an understanding of how the process works. When you bless or condemn something, your light body then becomes like a transmitter that emits a frequency to draw similar frequencies to you, so that you may choose to select what you want to bless or condemn next. Herein is the Law of Attraction at work. The point of attraction is created through your emotional field and your connected thoughts that draw things to you so that you can be free to make another choice. Unlike our human counterparts, there is nothing telling us what we must choose. Free choice is a blessing. And it is our birthright. Our work here is to deliberately make the point of attracting the reality we want to live.

Most people have no idea of the power one has through the art of blessing. This power is formidable; it can part the seas and create worlds. To develop the art of blessing is perhaps the easiest of all because blessing is a part of the very fabric of our being. You see, you were blessed into life and every cell of your being sings in harmony with the universe. If we can accept that what we say with emotion draws the reality forth from the undifferentiated matter of the universe, that we are indeed creators learning how to focus our formidable power, there is nothing out of our reach. Blessing is a deliberate and focused act of unconditional love. Learning to be a deliberate creator integrates the art of focused blessings to create the resonance to bring about the desired reality of your choice.

Once I found my voice as a singer of the language of light (similar to speaking in tongues), without fail, when I finished singing, people wanted to know where I learned to sing in that manner. A song in the language of light has a particular quality that is deeply moving. Early on, I could not respond clearly because I did not know how to explain. The feelings simply rose within me and I had to free them through my voice. Years later, I came to understand that my spiritual opening and the blessing I was able to bestow on others came from my own light body. The vibrations of the words that formed that realization shook the core of my being and brought forth a desire deep within me to heal the heart of humanity, which has been my motto all these years. I had no clue how that healing would happen, but what I did have was faith and trust in two things: first, in the blessings coming through me because of the way they made me feel, and second, seeing the reaction of the people who were touched by those same vibrations. We were all lifted and glowing from within because joy was present and as powerful as the blessings that rained upon us.

THE BLESSING EXPERIMENT

One weekend, at a gathering in my home, a couple from Billings, Montana, asked if they could do a special blessing over the food before we ate lunch. We were all accustomed to the ritual of blessing food, but their experience with blessing astounded us all.

The couple worked in a water treatment facility in Billings, where their job was to test toxic levels in the water from various cities around the United States. They proceeded to tell us about the water levels in different cities and how they were inspired to try something. Because they had access to state-of-the-art water-testing equipment, they wondered if they blessed the water, would the readings change? At the time, they said that the worst water in the country was in Kansas City and that is the reason they selected it to be their test for the measuring of the blessing. The experiment was simple: They held their hands over the beaker of water from Kansas City that had just tested poorly and sent out their heartfelt blessings into the water. Guess what? The water tested much better. They blessed the water one more time, and it tested perfectly. That was in 1983.

Many years later, we heard about another scientist, Masaru Emoto, and his experiments with the blessing of water. Through his inspiration and scientific experiments for many years, he maintained that human emotions alter the molecules in water. That emotion *is* joy activated and that emotional field from each one of us is transmitted, just like pheromones, without fail, through electrical frequencies and into the substances of our world. The idea that emotions *alter* the molecular structure of our physical reality is simply profound. Water is a great conductor. Joy asks that we love water, to appreciate it and use it for the well-being of our planet.

Most people have no idea of the power one has through the act of blessing.
This power is formidable; it can part seas and create worlds.

INTENTIONAL BLESSINGS

Blessings are intentions of well-being that are the underpinnings of life itself.

Both positive and negative emotions create the reality of our life experience. Each one of us has had experiences in our life that provide evidence to support the creative power of positive feelings. All of my experiences that I have shared with you have added immeasurably to my life and reach out to remind you of your own similar memories. Blessings are intentions of well-being that are the underpinnings of life itself. We are blessed beings on a blessed path of well-being, reawakening to the power of our ability to intentionally, deliberately create. Learning the art of blessing opens a secret doorway to the awareness of our eternal being, to energetic and vibrant health, to fulfilling and joyous relationships, to accepting each one of us as blessed beings. Can you feel the power in that?

As we mature and evolve in this beautiful life we have chosen to live, we begin to recognize that the first and foremost requirement of mastery is to consistently *bless all life. Do no harm.*

Breathe in the vibrational frequency of those statements; breathe it in because to understand the power of blessing is to realize the expansion of life everywhere. The energy of condemning is tight, resistant, unwilling, non-cooperative, forceful, coercive, resentful, divisive, imprisoning, and so on.

These statements have become so much a part of my life and my teachings that I want to share them with you:

Practice Blessing and Basking

- **Use the power of blessing** to bring you into alignment with joy, and all things good and very good will be gracefully drawn to you.

- **Blessing engages** both the Law of Resonance and the Law of Attraction to bring you closer to the reality you prefer.

- **Blessing offers appreciation,** which silences Yabbits and in turn serves as recognition that everyone is a master of his or her own creative expression.

- **Blessing allows room** for the expansion of who you are, and who you are becoming.

- **The Art of Blessing expands your light body,** touching everything with a blessed permission to live life according to whatever you might choose.

- **Blessing opens the door to greater awareness,** and deliberate choosing.

- **Blessing relieves you** of the pressure of believing that you can control another's behavior.

- **Blessing aligns you** with the source of your being, squarely placing you and me in the vortex of all things possible.

- **Blessing recognizes** not only your goodness, but also the goodness of life itself.

You are blessed, the world is blessed, and all is well.

Dr. Wayne Dyer, author of numerous self-help books, states as he teaches on intentions, "Learn to stop being offended." I had a chance to practice that concept when I received an e-mail from a student telling me she wanted to go in another direction, and would not be attending a class she had signed up for. This was someone I had great respect for and I was really looking forward to continuing our work together. Well, I felt I deserved more than a two-line e-mail and got properly offended, magically in the middle of writing this chapter. I was at the beach and decided to take a walk along the shoreline. Learn to stop being offended, off-ended, out of alignment, off my mark. Why? The next moment will bring in the icky-feeling Yabbits of self-righteous condemnation. Now what do I do?

As I walked, I watched hundreds of seagulls sitting on the beach, their beaks into the wind coming off the ocean, just watching, just being in the moment. They weren't offended so I decided to copy them, and sat on a bench with my face into the wind, just watching the waves coming in. I don't know what those gulls were thinking; I began to feel the wind, the fog, and the sprays of mist from the water. Then I felt empty of thought, and that felt good. Watching those gulls was fun, and I started to thank them for keeping the beaches clean, and before I knew it, I was in gratitude and appreciation for the wonderful time I was having. Actually, I realized that I was basking in the natural goodness I was witness to. As I did, I shifted and started thinking about breakfast.

When we bless, we align with the best within us,
and in the same way that clock wheels align,
blessings align us with the best of ourselves and others.

Take that a step further and give your blessing to what others choose to do. I know that this a big test for us all sometimes, but you must know that you are a "bringer" of light. I promise you that bringing light and reverently blessing the choices of others is not only tremendously rewarding, but it is also necessary. You are a bridge-builder. You are building bridges of consciousness that are evident everywhere. Even if others appear to cause harm and you become offended, see the best in them and bless their actions. Remember we are always at a place where we can choose. We can choose our thoughts, we can choose how we feel, and we can deliberately decide how to respond. As this process becomes more deliberate, it will free you to live your life consistently beyond limitations. You will no longer be imprisoned in unreasonable captivity by negative Yabbit attitudes.

As a teacher, there is a very important fact I must always keep in mind as I stand in front of a class of eager students—the class cannot go further than where I am in my creative genius space. And…miracles just love showing up to expand you further when you least expect them.

I was teaching a class in my church one evening to about 14 people when three men in ski masks came in. Their intention was to rob us. They made us take off our jewelry and take out our money. Without missing a beat, my co-teacher Roberta Zito and I began to bless the thieves, sending healing energy in the midst of their activities. There was a prayer we always said when negative energies were present: "Dear ones, you are healed and forgiven, you are connected to your Christ Self, and you are connected to your Christ Light. You are free from fear and pain; you are free from the Earth vibration. Go in peace...." Fearlessly, we gently chanted this prayer to each one of the thieves as they passed by gathering up our treasures. Soon, other students joined in and a wondrous thing happened...one thief began to apologize for disrupting our class; another left his bag on the floor as they left. We were all a bit shaken when the police came, and yes there were some lost possessions, but everyone was okay. The frequency from the Law of Resonance, coupled with the Law of Attraction and the effects of pure-hearted blessings from the group were truly amazing that night.

Experiment with this idea and watch what happens. Look into your stash of judgments, choose one, and deliberately begin to bless it. Pay attention: the power that blessing unleashes might astound you.

Creating your own reality is within
the structure of the Law of Attraction and is the basic premise of
how our universe operates.
Blessing is bestowed
from a generous heart,
a heart that sees only
eternal good
in
all things.

CHAPTER 9

GOODNESS IS OUR BIRTHRIGHT

SURELY GOODNESS AND MERCY SHALL FOLLOW YOU
ALL THE DAYS OF YOUR LIFE. NO MATTER WHERE I AM,
NO MATTER WHAT I MAY HAVE DONE OR AM DOING,
MY ESSENCE OF GOODNESS IS HELD INVIOLATE.

The idea of our inherent goodness, and the power contained within that idea, has inspired me so deeply that I have spent many years developing the Goodness Process through teaching its principles. The evidence is overwhelming every time. I find that people naturally gravitate toward their goodness, and the Yabbits rise to say, "Really?" My answer to those Yabbits is part of the blessings God gave as our birthright: "Surely goodness and mercy shall follow you all the days of your life" (Psalm 23:6). No matter where I am, no matter what I may have done or am doing, my essence of goodness is held inviolate.

This began some years ago when my husband Lee and I were vacationing on Mayne Island just off Vancouver Island. Because our Inner Focus community is always looking for an opportunity to connect, some of my beloved students and friends came over from Vancouver to join us for a meditation. In late July, the sun was bright in the Canadian sky until almost midnight. I loved the spot we chose, just above the water where you could hear all the sounds of the sea. The seals lazed in the sun, every now and again barking at one another. We each brought a favorite food dish to share, and enjoyed our gathering.

We meditated in the light, and were talking when I began to feel a familiar surge of energy deep within my heart. At this time, I had been a channel for many years, I knew the feeling, and the accompanying rush of energy, so as I became very aware of new thoughts pressing in, wanting to be a voice within this familiar group.

That day we had discussed our light body. I must admit I didn't know too much about what a light body was in those terms. I knew about auras, but I could sense there was a vast difference between the aura and the light body. They seemed different somehow from what I had already learned. And of course not wanting to miss a single thing, I was more than curious.

While in group meditation in Vancouver, my dear friend and mentor Jesus made Himself known, my channel opened, and in response to my curiosity, He had only these few words to say:

"Concentrate on your goodness, and your light body will build itself."

Wow! Absolutely profound! We were all excited, and could think of nothing else. When you hear a universal truth, you know it. The resonate frequency contained within the truth of the words themselves electrifies the auric field around you as the idea permeates your thoughts. Let's expand on the idea Seth introduced to us about how we create our own reality, because you can already sense the pattern of excitement forming here. The first step in creating your own reality is inspiration. Inspiration always comes forth from the centermost core of our being or what is now called Source energy. Inspiration is neutral; it is just a burst of joy that arrives from deep within us as we align with our greater self. Next are thoughts that erupt from that inspiration, and subsequent feelings that are encouraged from those thoughts, probably all crowding in at the same time. Everything is neutral up to that point. The burst of inspiration begs for a choice to be made.

Inspiration Creates
Your Reality

Thoughts and Emotions Create Possibilites

Centermost Core Inspiration
(Which Is Always Neutral)

Burst of Joy
Aligning With Your Greater Self

Thoughts Erupt and Create
a Resonance Frequency

Feelings Burst Forth as Indicators to
Lead to Your True Passion

Choice to Follow Passion

GOODNESS IN ACTION

The Goodness Process is fast because a vortex of joy comes in as a whirlwind of excitement. When you let yourself ride that wave, it will bring you success and happiness.

I presented a weekend class in New York City. Friday night was open to everyone, and the group was quite large. I did demonstrations that night on the goodness process. A woman, probably in her 50s, came up to the front. She expressed that she felt trapped in a well-paying job she really hated. We began the process that I will describe in detail later in this chapter. She was visibly altered when she left the podium only 15 minutes later. She was beaming, filled with self-confidence and hope. Although I never saw her again and I don't know her name, I know that through that brief moment with the Goodness Process, she was able to realize it was not the job she hated at all. She had hated herself. She grew up being told that she was bad and unworthy. Her true desire was a more creative role in her job, and she was afraid to let anyone know about it. By simply making the truth statement, "I am the essence of pure goodness," a resonate frequency was invoked within her that hushed the Yabbits, allowing her passion and her joy to activate, rise to the surface, and be fully known to her.

I AM the essence of pure goodness.

Goodness is our birthright. Joy is inherent in our goodness. Seth used to say, "You are a worthy, deserving person and you have a right to your place in this universe." I spent years contemplating that single thought. Now that I have embodied that teaching, I realize that having a right to my place in this universe means that no one, including me, has a right to rob me in any manner, through opinions, insults, or comments, of my birthright of worthiness, because it is all up to me and my perception that no one can take anything from me.

GETTING TO GOOD

After contemplation of the teaching, "Concentrate on your goodness, and your light body will build itself," the wonderful goodness process becomes a tool to work miracles and gets us powerfully on the track of activating our joy.

For many of us, a big problem is being able to believe in our own goodness. We can actively experience repetitive thought patterns that falsely state we are not worthy of much of anything. Our Yabbits reinforce these harmful thoughts and affect our belief system. Most of us have had the goodness trained out of us; to bring it back and reactivate it will require some inner focus.

The Goodness Process is a technique that uses soul awareness alignment to uncover and transform core shadow energies. Consciously connecting to the joy or positive intention that is present within a negative pattern, we can remind ourselves of our inherent, pure goodness. From this vantage point, we align with our essence, the Source of who we are, the good stuff.

As you continue the process, a powerful vortex of energy is created to heal chronic, life-long patterns quickly and gracefully without flashback.

When we are in pain, we make decisions about how to act or be, in order to resolve the problem we are facing and avoid feeling the pain. Yet still frozen in time, the original positive intention of that decision exists, and through alignment with and connection to the joyous truth of our pure goodness, this will bring us into alignment with the Source of our being. The false or shadowed ideas transform at a soul-level, relieving the pressure, and bringing in the light of goodness to bask in.

The Goodness Process

Before you begin, make sure you are not going to be interrupted. Turn off the ringer on your phone and put a "do not disturb" note on your door.

Next, create a pillar of light in the center of the room. You can do this through intention and visualization. Simply see a beautiful pillar of magnetic light and set the intention that this light will magnetically attract all negative energies for purification and release. Once the space is ready, align your thoughts.

Now align with your Source or Inner Self and do a short prayer or invocation to deepen the energy. This is the Inner Focus invocation that we have used for years in the school:

I AM the breath of God, my true and authentic self.

I breathe the heart of the earth.

I breathe the heart of the universe.

I am one with my soul.

I am one with my self.

My inner focus heals the heart of humanity.

Now that you are aligned and the space is focused on healing and upliftment, it is time to begin the five stages of the Goodness Process.

First Stage: Focusing Awareness

Focus your total awareness on the shadow pattern you want to heal. Feel the depth of your emotions. Example: "I'm afraid to let people see the real me…"

Breathe in the energy, and feel your resistance to allow others to see you. Pay attention to how the energy makes you feel. For example: Does it make you feel nothing, or do you go numb? Are you feeling uneasy or anxious, detached, not want-ing to look? Or perhaps it makes you queasy and feeling sick. The negative feeling will quickly become apparent, as it is your guidance system to feeling better.

Second Stage: Activating Soul Memory

Contemplate the word *goodness*. Your soul is the greater part of you, your Higher Self, the Source of you, and it remem-bers your birthright of goodness, even if you don't. Say this statement aloud: *I am the essence of pure goodness.*

Goodness is your essence.

This deep truth is the essence of your light body, and res-onates deeply within your cellular memory. No matter what you believe, or what anyone else has ever told you that later emerged as a belief, your goodness is held inviolate and waits for you to claim it for yourself.

As you focus the idea of goodness, you call forth your soul into your conscious awareness, deliberately, which automati-cally brings you into a state of grace. To be in a state of grace is to know that you are connected with well-being; it means that all good things surround you and flow naturally to you. You are never alone—your soul, God force, Source, whatever you want to call it, continually supports your personal well-being.

Your soul has a conscious awareness of your inherent goodness. The resonate frequency of goodness magnetically connects to all the negative Yabbit voices, such as, "You will never get it right; you will never be good enough. You are bad, and you have allowed yourself to believe in your badness and therefore lack of goodness."

These ideas survive unconsciously throughout your energy field and cause stress. You act them out unconsciously because they are not a natural part of you, and you want relief from them. And if the truth were known, they want to be relieved from this unpleasant task as well.

Third Stage: The Hands of "Goodness"

In the fist of one hand, hold your goodness. In the fist of the other hand, hold the energy of the belief you want to heal. Clench your fists tightly. Allow tension to build in your chest and body.

Feel the power created in the circle of energy that moves through your hands, arms, and chest. Your two fists represent the divine paradox you have been living in, the paradox of shadow and light. Say, "Today I am making a new choice."

Say the following statement out loud a few times: *I am the essence of pure goodness. My goodness has nothing to do with my actions or the actions of anyone else.*

Fourth Stage: Alignment and Transformation

Continue to hold that position into this next stage. The mudras or hand positions are meant to build the energy needed to release the negative thoughts. As you experience the tension in your arms and chest, feel the tension in your life. The goodness statement brings relief and hope. Within a short time, the energies that are blocking the acceptance of your goodness begin to rise into conscious awareness so you can hear them, and then let them go.

Build up your power base of goodness by going back and forth from one hand to the other, with your goodness statement in one hand and then the negative reply in the other. Follow this example: *I am the essence of pure goodness* versus *It's dangerous to show people who I am.*

Then, in the height of your emotions, bring your hands together in front of your heart, placing one hand over the other, and say with gusto, out loud: *It's all the same one thing!*

This is the clincher! Hold this pose for a few minutes, realizing that the position of your hands takes you beyond the belief systems of the mind. Because your birthright of goodness is larger and more potent than the scared Yabbit, goodness embraces the negative and diffuses the Yabbit energy. This is cellular. The transformational hand gesture reminds the body that it doesn't have to stay limited and separated, that it can return to a natural state of unity and wholeness. Trust what is happening. Trust joy! Claim your own authority.

Fifth Stage: Appreciation and Gratitude

To transmute something is to change its inherent quality. When the idea that "I am inherently bad" is realized to be a profoundly false concept, your Inner Being changes exponentially on every level. The "ah ha" is so strong that it can often be felt physically.

Feel the upliftment. Feel the changes occurring within you. Appreciate yourself, the energy, the angels, the masters who have helped by holding the space of truth for you. The truth is that it is all good, that goodness is within everything, no matter what it may look like or what you may have done. Mostly appreciate yourself for your courage to allow conscious awareness to guide you into your true self. Appreciation and gratitude are now in this very moment expanding your energy on every level and your light body is glowing.

Maintenance of Your Goodness Connection

Now that you have experienced the Goodness Process, ask yourself: *How do I see my new sense of goodness being reflected in my life? What will change?*

Let your thoughts flow, and imagine the most wonderful, most expansive, and most joyously freeing experience possible. You are the master you seek and the only authority worth paying attention to.

In the beginning, the idea that I was the essence of pure goodness was so strong I needed to prove it to myself over and over again. I guess that was my way of practicing the power of this most amazing understanding. When you hear a truth that resonates with you, it is always necessary to entrain yourself to the new vibration.

I made goodness cards the size of business cards and carried them with me, reading them whenever I needed a goodness reminder. I made up songs and poems about my goodness. I think the most important statement was and still is for me that I am the essence of pure goodness no matter what I have done or what I think anyone else has done to me. Can you feel the relief of a lifetime of guilt that this new understanding releases for you?

For me, personally, I knew this would be a major teaching that I would bring into the world and I wanted to teach from my own experience of working this process with myself and others. After all these years, I still feel this single process is all anyone needs to align with the greatest power within them.

You are the master you seek and the only authority worth paying attention to.

This Goodness Process might take a few tries; stick with it, and before long, your Yabbits will be disempowered and that good feeling, the part of you that knows your goodness and has always believed in you, will get stronger and stronger. Happiness will invade your life, lifting your heart, relaxing your thoughts.

Benefits of the Goodness Process

- ❧ You benefit by becoming more self-centered, aware, and focused in the truth of you.

- ❧ You learn to care about how you feel about yourself.

- ❧ You find that you value your own thoughts and ideas.

- ❧ In the process of retraining, you discover that you are and always have been the one in power.

- ❧ Wonderful feelings of exciting, joyous peace permeate your experience.

- ❧ You want every day to be filled with joy.

- ❧ Now, when you feel discord, reach for your goodness and all else will be added unto you.

Relax and let happiness invade your life. Joy is the beholder of joy.

Combining awareness of your Yabbits with using the Goodness Process, you begin to reestablish the pathways of joy that, as deliberate creators, are imperative for us right now. Activate joy and remember all things happy. Trust your instincts as you uncover joy in as many instances as possible.

CHAPTER 10

THE CHALLENGE OF BEING DEBT-FREE

WHEN YOU CAME INTO THIS WORLD, JOY RUSHED IN WITH YOUR FIRST BREATH AND BUBBLED WITH AN EFFERVESCENCE THAT DELIGHTED EVERYONE.

Being free from debt is being free from worry and fear. *Free* is the operative word in this chapter. The joy that comes from being debt-free is being free to *be* yourself and allowing others to do the same. Now that is a challenge.

Let's define debt as I am using it in this chapter: energetic obligations, emotional burdens that make us feel as though we are falling short of the mark, or are not quite good enough. When we begin to open a new awareness of how energetic debt is created, we discover that the energy of debt sets up a resonate field filled with similar energy, which activates the Law of Attraction to create the very experiences we *don't* want.

The truth is, we are hard-wired to create debt of one sort or another because this attracts contrasting experiences that result in our expansion into greater self-awareness. The challenge is to become aware of the sometimes subtle differences so we can deliberately choose the reality we prefer.

It is my intention to uncover the most hidden of agendas within the idea of creating debt; because debt, like grief, can keep you from being able to connect with joy. We know how we get into debt financially, but do you know how you incur energetic debt?

Any author will tell you that in the process of writing a book on any subject, deep insights and transformations take place. My insight happened when I was looking at the challenge of becoming debt-free. Much of what I learned is included in this chapter.

Because we are familiar with the Goodness Process, let us use the power of the paradoxical world (the world of opposites) we have already explored and now have more awareness to show us the opposite thought to the one we are holding. As I pondered the phrase, *I want to be debt-free,* I heard familiar rhetoric (the Yabbits) reminding me how bad I am. To empower ourselves even more, we might employ the phrase: *My goodness is in the debt I have created through falsely believing that I could be unworthy in any way. I am the essence of pure goodness and my goodness has nothing to do with my actions or the actions of anyone else.* Say this a few times and then watch for the Pleaser Yabbits as they form their committee to make their shame-based case of objections.

I notice that negative thoughts often come in clusters; many connected thoughts are centered on the same theme, all clamoring to be heard at the same time. To transform entrenched feelings of unworthiness, which negative self-esteem is geared to support, one must be convinced that: first, it's okay to accept your inherent goodness; second, you are willing to be powerful and steer the course of your own life; and third, you want to be able to feel good about yourself all the time. And in those times when you don't feel good about yourself, be aware that you have knowledge of how to activate your joy.

I was brought up in a home with parents who were wonderful in many ways and also believed whole-heartedly in "spare the rod and spoil the child." Although I was mostly a very happy little girl, I emerged into adulthood with underlying beliefs that something was wrong with me, I didn't measure up, and I was unworthy in some way. These ideas led me straight into a pattern of needing to prove myself to everyone, and so this pattern continued for most of my young life and far into adulthood. When you think you need to prove yourself to anyone, you create emotional debt. Always looking for love, energetically, you falsely think you owe someone a part of you. You think you have to prove that you are worth something to make it okay to even exist. You think you need someone else to be happy because you are never enough.

Nullify the debt of suffering by deliberately choosing throughout the day to be happy.

So if I think I need to prove myself, I am undervaluing me, I'm not worth believing in, and I may continually chase the need to prove myself, so that somehow I can feel of some value. Sometimes it can get convoluted to the point that you are trying to prove to yourself that you have a right to be alive. Exhausting!

I spent a lot of energy contemplating and studying, trying and striving in vain to figure out how to become completely debt-free. Wow, what a challenge that is, and did I ever experience a big *ah-ha* when I finally got it...I realized that it is in our nature to attract contrasting experiences so that we may grow and learn how to deliberately choose which experiences we truly want to live with.

I wondered if it is possible to be completely debt-free. Because this is a rather challenging thought, but one I feel is in front of everyone, given the circumstances bombarding us in our outward reality these days, I felt it important to include in this writing. The power of understanding the energetics of debt is that this knowledge can lead us to realize our own inherent self-value and appreciate the equity we have amassed through the experiences we have lived. The key here is to note the *great* difference in the debt created intentionally versus naively created when we let things get out of hand, as in obsessive thinking. Life and joy activated are in a constant state of forward movement; holding on to the debt of angry feelings creates contracted energy, pain, and suffering. By deliberately choosing the reality you prefer through deliberate focus on that subject, you actually begin the process of living in the reality you want. This is a challenge because we have been trained to focus in the opposite direction. Staying focused on a positive outcome takes tenacity and practice.

Look at the emotional trips parents lay on us. "This is my house and these are the rules; you are a guest in my house so you better do what I say, or else." The inference in that example is that there is a debt owed, and subconsciously you wonder if you can ever pay that back. Our belief systems are littered with insurmountable debt that we are completely unaware of. From a very early age, for many of us, our self-worth is all encumbered with debt. Some may read this and think, "Isn't that what parents are supposed to do? Aren't they required to raise children with the awareness of rules and good behavior?" In the old paradigm, that was our training, however when we look at some of the outcomes, perhaps it is time to amend some of our parenting "guidelines" through a greater awareness.

I will tell you what began to erase the greater part of this emotional debt for me. Many years ago, I was at a popular self-improvement seminar. The discussion came up about loving parents and I erupted like Mount Vesuvius. Years of being a pleaser and doing everything in my power to prove myself to my mother and father unleashed an unreasonable rage from deep within me that flew all over the room. This rage came from years of being belittled and berated for not being good enough in school, for being chubby, for never measuring up to whatever my parents thought I should be doing. Because my father was very strict, I had learned how to be as quiet as a mouse, hoping no one would notice me, because when he did, there was no mercy. My home was reflective of many homes; there are periods of anger and upheaval and periods of really joyful experiences. I was starting to realize that, as a child, I couldn't understand the contrast between upheaval and joy; plus, I thought the upheaval was my fault. The leaders of the group were masterful and allowed me to be as upset as I needed to be until, just a little while later, it was suddenly over.

The leader said something so powerful to me that it changed my perspective on my relationship with my parents forever. He said, "You will always love your parents because they gave you life, but no one says you have to like them if they treated you badly." I remember feeling as though ice cold water had been thrown in my face. It took a day and a half before I could talk to anyone. The weight that lifted off of me that day was palpable.

DEBT FREE! I don't owe anything to anyone and I don't have to earn my worthiness.

Apparently, I had visibly changed, because many people commented on it. I don't owe anything to anyone and never did. Because of that realization, I can practice making a deliberate choice to be debt-free of my parents' demands that somehow remained active. My self-esteem went way up because I was now able to place more value in myself than trying to prove myself, or thinking I needed to do something to make anyone proud of me just so I could feel loved. I don't owe anyone anything and I don't have to earn my worthiness! In fact, I am learning through the Law of Attraction that I don't have to earn anything. I simply need to follow my bliss and everything I want, everything I deliberately choose to resonate with, will be attracted to me.

THE RESONANCE OF DEBT AND VALUE

The Law of Resonance and the Law of Attraction work in tandem. The resonance of debt is at the crux of financial woes and so many other issues that gather around us, or are attracted to us, that beg for our attention on a daily basis. Financial challenges are biggies that can unplug your *joy*—and *fast*. It is hard to be positive and attract more of what you want when you have no money to buy groceries. Yes, food is an urgent, immediate need; however, we want to get to the root of the challenge creating the resonance that results in the situation in which you can't afford groceries. The apex is found when, despite all circumstances, you have the ability to flow into a resonating field that will help you attract the means to receive the nourishment you are seeking, or that which you truly desire.

You are worth a lot, and you have grown in value because of the equity that has built up within your very being.

To find the root, let's look at the classic idea of debt-to-value ratio with a different perspective. Let's think of ourselves as "equitable" (value), meaning that throughout the years you have "acquired" (asset) meaningful knowledge, in that you have been able to make a living with the knowledge you have gained. Then you have also gained the wisdom (asset) to make better and better choices with that knowledge (value). You are worth a lot, and you have grown in value because of the equity that has built up within your very being. Please take that statement in.

Perhaps it is time to redefine our own intrinsic value rather than be told what "it" is that we should value. In order for others to value you, you have to value yourself. In this process, you will learn the power of self-appreciation, which is akin to self-love.

How Do I Accept My Personal Value?

Your self-esteem equals your personal value system. You were created from joy and joy has been a directive force in developing your self-esteem. You knew you were worthy of having anything you wanted until the voices said, "No, you can't." Self-esteem is a necessary component to thriving, and you will get it any way you can—either through positive or negative reinforcement.

For me, I discovered that, by being a pleaser, I devalued myself so that I could feel good about something. After working with the idea of negative and positive self-esteem, and teaching its principles for many years, I discovered different components that could easily be identified that would help in the acceptance of personal value. Through these processes, I was able to make definable choices that helped me to see value in myself, and through my transformation, I was able to share those methods with others.

One of the Yabbits' tricks is to make us feel bad about ourselves (shame-based negative self-esteem). In my case, I condemned myself for everything; I devalued myself. Of course if I devalued me, then I had to devalue others, as well as finding fault with any little thing. Do you see how this works? By seeing flaws in others, it somehow makes you feel better. In a strange way there was acceptance from others because they were doing the same thing. After a while, you realize it really does not work out so well. Complaining about anything is negative self-esteem.

Reaching for joy beyond that Yabbit I began to be truthful about how I really felt about a subject, even though it scared me a lot. As a child, telling the truth might have meant being punished: that fear was energetic debt I carried with me. As I gained confidence, I was more honest about my true feelings, and discovered I really did have good principles, which then developed into a high sense of integrity. Because I valued myself, claiming my power by being honest became easier and easier.

Once you take responsibility for creating that particular way of being—without condemning yourself in any way—then you can learn to focus on positive self-esteem. The more you deliberately choose positive feelings, the results exponentially multiply upon themselves. Herein is the secret of living beyond limitations: All limitations are self-imposed, and if you created it, you can change it. You are the only one who can. Reactivating your natural base of divine worthiness will simply take a short amount of time as you practice feeling good about yourself, and taming the clamoring Yabbits into cheerleaders.

Self-esteem is our most powerful source for accepting divine worthiness. Self-esteem is one issue that cannot be avoided as we lift our consciousness, and achieve higher levels of spiritual maturity. Self-esteem must be transformed by you through the conscious awareness of your own sense of values, new values you are learning through this process.

When you came into this world, you knew who you were; joy rushed in with your first breath and bubbled with an effervescence that delighted everyone as you grew up. Then the rules, and the way the rules were explained to you, slowly dimmed your delight. Did picking flowers become a no-no? Or playing in the rain? Or was climbing a tree too dangerous? Were you the one who was not chosen by your classmates to be on the team? Were sweets not allowed?

It might seem that going back to sift through the Yabbit world can become a daunting task, but you will soon discover how easy it can be. Because you have already done the preparation work in the previous chapters, the rewards will be amazing. Through all that I know and all that I have become, my blessing to you is to be debt-free by knowing that when you incur a debt through contrast that you recognize it immediately, and bounce into a debt-free space. You never have to relive negative experiences. You never need to chew on old hurts when you realize they are in fact rubber walls there for you to bounce against. In doing this, you can live the joyous life you came here to live.

SHIFTING OUR PERSPECTIVE OF VALUE

"Deliberately and consciously choose to value yourself" is a paradigm shift statement I must credit the Abraham-Hicks material for bringing into the light of day. This was one piece of the puzzle that had been lost for me and I'll bet for many others as well. The moment I heard this truth statement it resonated throughout my being and I felt the freedom of the ages lift off of me.

We can get hooked on the premise that we should always put others before us. In doing this, it would seem that we would be more worthy...of what? To exist? I'm not sure. This is a really confusing and misunderstood concept that has, for thousands of years, entranced many religions, cultures, and societies. Times are changing. Toes are just getting wet, veils are lifting, and consciousness is expanding into a greater expectancy of joy. Could we be coming into the time our forefathers predicted, the time we pound our weapons into plowshares? We can do both. We can value ourselves and understand how important our feeling good about what we are choosing to do is. In so doing, it serves those we want to help as well.

We will always create energetic debt of one sort or another because the contrast, the choices we have to make, cause us to expand into greater self-awareness one way or another. Valuing yourself creates a clearer perspective, and this causes you to be more discerning about the choices you are making. The foundation of your choice needs to be for you so the benefit is there for all. Here's the first question you have to ask yourself: *Do I really want to do this?* Immediately check your emotional response. Does it feel good?

If you unconsciously say yes because you think it will make someone
else happy,
the debt of resentment begins. Yuck.
If you follow your joy and go in the direction of your
best and highest feelings, you will be debt-free. Ahh.
Choosing joy changes everything!

Value yourself more each day; trust your internal guidance system to point you toward the good feelings before you make agreements. Appreciate yourself and your ability to know what is right for you. Trust other people. This is the paradigm shift that is occurring right now and we are turning the tide...so be easy with yourself. Everything is going to work out perfectly; start with small things and then when a big choice comes up, your practice will pay off.

Each process in *Activate Joy* has been leading to this important moment. As you learn to accept your value and allow the fabric of goodness to hold and enfold you, realizing that this has always been the deep truth of our being, joy will activate within you. You will not be able to hold back as the vortex of joy sweeps you up.

Value, Worthiness, Trust: Positive Self-Esteem in Action

While teaching a seminar, a process spontaneously came through in response to a student trying to understand why she did not feel worthy of being successful. When I asked her what she valued about herself, she couldn't relate to being valuable at all. As we worked through a succession of questions, it was such a profound experience that I had to include it in *Activate Joy*. This process will help you become more aware of your own self-value. From there, you will face challenges and create debt in your life that will actually help you as you live your life beyond limitations.

Value

Focus on your value. Notice that you value yourself in very specific ways.

Take a moment to make a list of the following:

1. What do you value about yourself?

2. What do you value about your body?

3. What do you value about your intelligence?

4. What is the most important thing you appreciate about yourself?

Take a moment as the joy of self-value activates and list other things that you value about yourself. Don't be shy.

If you do not see your value, you cannot know your worthiness. When you do not know your value, you cannot share who you truly are; you will only share what others have told you about yourself, and taught you that it is safe to share. So this step is very important. When you value yourself, what you have to say, and your decisions in life, your heart is lighter; there is no debt mounting up, and all resistance to joy becomes irrelevant.

Valuing everything about the life you have chosen to live and the physical being that you are is key. Learning to appreciate where you are and where you want to go is the energy of alignment. Value all of the choices you have made, knowing each one moved you into a new and empowering experience.

Say the following words aloud to yourself. Feel free to add other words and statements that reflect you.

Activating Value Alignment #1

I appreciate my value in new and empowering ways. It feels so good to know that I have value. I love knowing that I can share myself, and feel good about who I am. I so appreciate who I am, and what I bring to the world. I love knowing my value, and allowing myself to express my magnificence. It is so relaxing to know that I know my value. I feel freedom coursing through my veins. I feel my cells aligning with the joy of life. I experience awakening to knowing my value and sharing myself with others, unafraid. Through knowing my value, I am willing to participate in life on all levels. I love participating. When I participate, I feel joyful."

Through misunderstanding of self-value, we create a holding pattern when mesmerized by the glamour of outer reality. A gap is created. The more we believe physical reality is real, the wider and wider the gap becomes. Greater and greater energetic debt mounts in front of us; mountainous debt that creates fear and often panic over the overwhelming evidence of lack and limitation. We temporarily forget that the source of life is vibrational, non-physical, and eternal. Our focus shifts to the physical indications of what seems real, rather than the expansion of what we originally intended to experience. When stuck, and focused on what is missing, it makes us feel terrible, leading us to take class after class, or go on a quest for some secret formula outside ourselves, until one day, finally, the discomfort is so strong, we make a deliberate choice for an inner focus to pay attention to what we want, what we desire, in order to bring back joy in our lives; to love and appreciate who we truly are right now.

Each time we value our self and the good feelings associated with personal upliftment and self-appreciation, we connect to joy; the gap closes, and the debt dissolves into nothing.

Conscious deliberate choice builds upon itself continually. Enlightenment into our true value generates even more knowing.

Activating Value Alignment #2

I am learning to value myself, to treasure the moments I can spend with myself. Any debt creating a weight that at times has become unbearable is released as I become free. It is easy for me to deconstruct any and all belief systems that would not serve me and would cause more negative debt. Aligning with my value allows me the freedom to speak with unconditional love for others and myself. To be vulnerable strengthens trust in myself. I appreciate who I am. When I value myself, I value others as cooperative components mirroring exactly what I need to be aware of in the moment. Because I create my own reality, I only create goodness, no matter what the reality may look like. This being true, only goodness can come to me.

Worthiness: You Are a Worthy, Deserving Person

Worthiness is a direct result of loving and valuing yourself as a person. Worthiness is a given. You are a worthy, deserving person because you are *alive*—you exist.

This knowledge is pivotal to the challenge of freeing ourselves from debt because most of us have challenges when it comes to self-worth. Most of us have been trained by society to view worthiness through the eyes of achievement, success in one form or another. The brave ones who were deemed non-conformists, those who could not deny a passion to follow their dream wherever it might lead had to ride on their birthright of worthiness. Mostly it was not conscious or understood as worthiness, but a driving creative force that one simply had to value and then follow wherever it led them.

To activate your birthright of worthiness, begin by appreciating your life, all the paths that have led you to this very moment, the crooks in the road and the dawn of inspiration that made you turn in another direction. Worthiness begets self-love, hope for what is to come. Worthiness allows authentic power, and realizes the extreme power of valuing yourself just because.

Say the following words aloud to yourself. Feel free to add other words and statements that reflect you.

Activating Worthiness Alignment

I so appreciate that knowing is of high value to me. Knowing establishes confidence and erases potential debt. When I am in the knowing of my value, it is easy for me to believe in myself, and I feel worthy. As I focus on my inner knowing and trust my own guidance, I am strengthened in the realization of divine worthiness for me and everyone else.

I am a deliberate creator and I KNOW who I am, and in this knowing, awareness opens me to the vaults of universal knowledge that now want to be expressed through me in a new and greater way. I accept that I am limitless. I allow universal abundance into my life experience. I align with my eternal nature of worthiness and I know it.

When I know who I am, it is easy to stop the process of the accumulation of accidental debt.

Trust: Focus Trust in You

Take a few moments and slowly contemplate trust.

- ೋ Trust evolves through valuing yourself and knowing your worthiness.

- ೋ Trust lives in the heart of innocence.

- ೋ Trust expects nothing from others.

- ೋ Trust allows truth to be known.

- ೋ Trust allows intimacy.

- ೋ Trust is faith in action

- ೋ Trust lives in neutral territory.

- ೋ Trust supports freedom.

- ೋ Trust knows well-being.

- ೋ Trust knows wealth.

- ೋ Trust knows all.

All of this knowledge is within you. You did come with a manual and it is written upon your heart. When you use your breath and connect with the greatest within you, that is who you are, these words that have been written upon these pages come to life for you, waiting to be lived by you.

We are not a society of haves and have-nots. We are a society of haves. Nothing is out of our reach. Nothing is too good to be true. All it takes is for you to believe and just let go. See things as yours, and then reach out and allow yourself to have them.

Say the following words aloud to yourself. Feel free to add other words and statements that reflect you.

Activating Trust Alignment

When I trust myself, I know my value and my worthiness. I understand that I am an eternal being and that everything is always going to work out well for me. I am joyous in the knowledge that all I have to do is to trust myself like the dolphins trust the water as they glide effortlessly and playfully on their way. I am finding it easier to trust my feelings and move in the direction of what makes me feel good. I am joyously anticipating the next experience, wondering what surprises await me. I have faith that something new and wonderful will show itself as my natural next step. I now find it easy to speak what is on my mind so as not to incur debt. I focus on feeling my abundance, knowing wealth is who I am.

There is an energetic pinnacle being reached that is causing this next shift. You and I are part of the cause of this effect through our determination to be all that we can be, to be in joy and goodness, blessing our entire journey.

Choose to be a deliberate creator.

Be aware.

We are ready to joyfully face the blessing of success
and great wealth;

we are ready to say yes to our birthright of unbridled abundance.

Nothing is out of our reach.

Nothing is too good to be true.

All it takes is for you to believe in yourself
and allow it to happen.

See things as yours
and then reach out
and allow yourself to have them.

You deserve it!

You don't have to work hard or struggle when you follow your heart and activate joy. Allow excitement and passion to lead the way and life just gets easier and easier.

CHAPTER 11

TUNING IN TO THE JOY CHANNEL

TRUST THAT THE GREATER PART OF YOU KNOWS
EXACTLY WHAT YOU WANT AND NEED, AND BRINGS IT
TO YOU IMMEDIATELY.

We are all connected to the Source of Life itself. Everyone uses their innate abilities to bring forth inspiration from deep within all the time. Some of us have less resistance than others. Channeling is a focused tuning, reaching a higher frequency than we are used to using on a daily basis. This frequency is usually tuned in to our Higher Self or Soul, broadcasting on an inspirational wavelength.

I am fascinated with the idea of fine-tuning our "receptors" to the higher frequency of joy. Activating spontaneous feelings of upliftment and well-being can become our normal way of life. To help us understand this concept more fully, we only need to look at how technology is mirroring the depth and breadth of our expansion. Let's look at television, for example. Remember when it was necessary to use "rabbit ears" to get a good reception? Remember the silver foil and having to mess with them to hopefully get a clear picture? Reminds me of messing with those pesky Yabbits to fine-tune our feelings; are they my beliefs or yours? Or how about those early computers? Who ever heard of WiFi? Yet it was just a few short years ago that broadband reception and high-definition televisions were introduced. Today these high-tech components are readily accepted and much more affordable.

Now, can you accept that our improved technology is mirroring our ability to receive information? Have you experienced these changes, too? I find that many people have been rewired and upgraded to high-definition reception. Now, I also realize that in so doing we have activated our pre-frontal cortex, the higher aspect of our brain. These receptors in the brain are way beyond anything we now call "broadband." This part of our brain is the part we have been awakening for years, incrementally crawling, walking, running, and now flying within the dimensional frequencies of light and joy, releasing endorphins that unleash rushes of healing tones that cause the physical cells of our body to align immediately with their innate perfection, uncoiling the ancient kundalini energy center of the spine to bring greater clarity and higher awareness into our everyday experience. Just like watching high-definition TV or surfing the Internet with a WiFi connection, perfect health and creative success are easily reachable, right now.

Understanding the Idea of Channeling

First of all, I invite you to realize that reaching for what is already inside you and waiting for you is easy to get to. With practice, accessing this information becomes effortless. It is like we become Olympic athletes who train to focus so completely that there are no distractions; no other voices contradicting the knowledge that we will indeed reach our goal. With training, everything in the body obediently comes into alignment, anticipating the joy of victory.

Throughout the years, I have been contacted by many consciousness beings that want to be heard, trying out their understanding through me. Throughout my years of teaching people how to allow the messages from other dimensions to come through, I have some simple guidelines that always work.

Any message you receive needs to have all three of these components to be assured of the clear content of the message:

1. Unconditional love
2. Non-judgment
3. Equality

These are easy ways to become aware if there is any subconscious pushing occurring. When I encounter that in myself or others I simply stop, realign, and ask for greater clarity.

In this book, I give you examples of the greatest channels I have ever listened to and that have inspired me. The teachings that continue to inspire me as I learn and grow is to know we are all in this together, equally; we are all masters in our own right, we each have a unique focus, and we can tune in to any frequency or channel with which we choose to align our thoughts.

As we enter new and expanded degrees of awareness, perhaps the idea of channeling might seem passé for some. The reason I mention it is that it was and still is my path and helps me better understand not only my life, but also life on all levels. As a teacher, healer, and mentor, it is my job to be able to align with the needs and desires of those I am supporting with expanded awareness.

What Is Channeling?

Channeling is simply relaxing my own thoughts and possible projections, which allows the inspiration already present in the client or student to come to the surface and be known. I hold the focus, which in turn transmits the loving and nonjudgmental energy for them to tune their frequency to. The results are miraculous in many cases. In the old paradigm, channels spoke for others. The new, much expanded paradigm allows a channel, such as myself, to empower others to realize their own truth. The rewards for all are astounding.

Because we all channel and bring forth information from deep within, what type of channel do you see yourself as? Can you think of yourself in those terms? In times of crisis, are you an uplifter? When someone really needs help, do you find that you are saying just the perfect things that help him or her feel better? During those moments when it seems that you're daydreaming, do you realize that you are accessing the potential to draw inspirational ideas and thoughts to you? As you realize the power in these moments, and with practice, you can deliberately create an atmosphere of receptivity with the intention of allowing your Inner Being to bring you a teaching. This teaching can be on anything, and you don't have to get specific at first. Trust that the greater part of you knows exactly what you want and need and will bring it to you immediately.

I discovered my channeling abilities in Elmira, New York while attending Seth classes with Jane Roberts and her husband Rob Butts in the early 1970s. Jane was a trance-medium. This type of channeling means that Jane's consciousness left her body while she allowed the being known as Seth to give teachings to us and to the world through her. When we asked Jane where she went while she channeled Seth, she always answered, "I don't know, playing somewhere I guess."

In the old paradigm, channels spoke for others. The new, much expanded paradigm allows a channel, such as myself, to empower others to realize their own truth. The rewards for all are astounding.

My Weekly Drive to Elmira

When I share that I knew Jane Roberts, people are curious and ask me what it was like to be in those early classes on Water Street, so I want to describe what that was like.

At the time of our first awakening, there are momentous moments and magical days. In the fall of 1972, I had written to Jane to tell her how much reading *The Seth Material* had changed my life. She had been channeling Seth since 1963 and asked one of her participants, Richie, to call me just to communicate her appreciation. Richie and I talked and had many long conversations about the goings-on within the weekly ESP classes. One day Richie told me that Jane would like to invite me to come. After much discussion, it was decided that I would go, and Lee was all for it. And because I had a Lincoln Continental that I and four others could all fit into, I would drive. Jane dubbed my passengers "the boys from New York." For approximately 18 months, everyone met at my home in Riverdale, New York, at 1 p.m. on Tuesday, and we took off on the five-hour drive to Elmira. The interesting part for me was that we drove through my hometown of Vestal, and that was a compelling connection for me. The weekly class began at 7:30 and we wanted to make sure we got there early enough to get a seat on the couch; otherwise we would sit on the floor for the entire session.

Jane Roberts and Rob Butts were great people who lived in a modest apartment in an old house on Water Street in Elmira. They heartily welcomed the large group into their small apartment, probably around 25 to 30 people squeezed into their living room once a week. During the sessions I attended, Jane was in the process of writing *The Nature of Personal Reality*, and so the first few hours of the sessions were spent in discussion with the people attending on subjects such as dreams, probable realities, and ESP work. Jane liked drinking her wine and smoked cigarettes constantly during our discussions. The group was made up of mostly rowdy young men, and it was always fun. Class usually ended around midnight and the boys and I took turns driving back to Riverdale where their cars were parked. We had lots of intellectual discussions on every topic you could imagine. Over the year and a half that I attended her sessions, I had some extreme experiences. Seth taught us how to work with the weather, and I was having great fun in New York City one day stopping the rain so I could dart across the street. Here is the secret Seth gave us: You simply ask the weather angels permission to give you what you want. Sometimes they can't and you have to allow for that, but most of the time they did. One example all of my students will tell you is that I usually bring the sunshine with me, especially to Madison, Wisconsin, in the winter. Another surprising experience was "hearing" the voices of unborn babies in their mothers' wombs.

TUNING IN

It was with Seth that I really discovered and began to develop my channeling abilities, by working with babies ready to come into this reality and also with people who were ready to pass away, back into non-physical. To this day, I often hear the voices of babies still in their mother's womb. Several times they really wanted to be called by a specific name and would call out their name (their vibrational song) until I spoke it out loud. One day I was working with Geraldine, a member of my congregation. She was worried about her new granddaughter who was born with an ear infection that would not go away. At five months, they were worried that she would lose her hearing altogether if the doctors could not clear it up. And she cried all the time. As I tuned in to the baby she said, "I won't hear that name!" Geraldine told me the parents had named her Alice after a family member. I asked the baby what name she wanted to be called. When I spoke her preferred name out loud, Geraldine began to cry. It seems grandma also resonated with the name. After several weeks of the family using the preferred name, the ear infection cleared up. The parents changed the baby's name officially and all was well. Every time I tell that story, I am blessed by the now grown woman. I also recognize that experience solidly anchored my confidence in my channeling abilities.

DO YOU have the suspicion that you are a cooperative component, and an essential part of something greater than yourself?

Someone asked me if I knew I was witnessing history with Seth and if I realized how special it was to be among the very few to have been called to those gatherings. Yes and no. I had a suspicion that perhaps I was a part of something greater than myself because we had to drive through my hometown of Vestal every week. I was aware enough to know that when we choose to come into this reality, we often come in clusters of friends and family, and that we often live in close proximity to one another. The other clue for me was that my interests and Jane's connected in many ways. I was an artist, which is how it happened that Jane invited me in the first place. And of course Rob, her husband, was also an artist. In my letter to her, I wrote that I had been teaching a small group of people how to paint apples with oil paints. These people professed not to know how to draw a straight line. Because I believed wholeheartedly that I indeed created my own reality, it seemed to me I was invincible. I told her that I had developed a special technique of mixing colors so no one could mess up and create mud, and that I was studying Cezanne's method of painting apples, and further, that my little group was doing a splendid job. Jane had an interest in many of the great writers and painters and later wrote a book, *The World View of Paul Cezanne: A Psychic Interpretation*.

Being with Jane and Rob and with all the special people of that day seemed so natural to me. And no, I had no idea of the magnitude of the teaching and the opening that would later reveal itself as the foundation to the great expansion we are experiencing today. However, in retrospect, as I recall the power of those days in my life, I am humbled in deep appreciation for the alignments that took place then and now. Reliving those times allows joyous as well as reverent memories to come alive again. New words and understandings of phrases such as *cooperative components* from Abraham-Hicks sparkle within my reverie.

Did I tell others what I was doing? Yes I did, especially my dearest friend Carol. Carol was a very special person in my life. She was always very positive and, like me, just loved to laugh. Our kids were about the same age when we met, and we played tennis and sat in the park at Skyview apartments in Riverdale, New York, almost every day. I am sure she thought I was a little goofy, but she listened with great interest as I recounted the events of my weekly trips to Elmira. Jane often talked to us about a book she read or some experience she had. One evening she read from a book called *Strange Experiences* by Lee Raus Gandee and talked about magical powers and such. There was one passage in the book that recounted using a Bible passage to stop excess bleeding. Of course I had to read the book immediately. Several weeks later, Carol called me to tell me that her father had a burst aorta and was not expected to live. As I listened, I felt a deep knowing that he would not die, and I told her that. When we got off the phone, I immediately went to the Bible passage and used the words to bless and visualize the stopping of his bleeding. I remember awaking in the early morning hours and seeing Carol's father, whom I had never met, sitting at the bottom of my bed. He just smiled at me for a long time and then winked. I knew he would be okay and I couldn't wait to tell Carol. You can imagine her response: "I know you really believe all of this stuff, but really…" I continued to speak the words of the Bible verse every night. And every so often, Carol's father would visit me and sit on the edge of my bed and smile at me. Then, before he left, he would wink, letting me know he was okay. Of course I recounted these events to Jane the next week as we were discussing Extra

Sensory Perception (ESP), and being able to recognize thought forms and such. In a certain degree of innocence I just accepted it all without any doubt as to the validity of the experience.

One day, right after he had paid me a visit, Carol called to say she had to go to Florida, that her father was dying and they were going to take him off life support. I told her I would go with her to Florida and we left that next morning. I continued to feel this deep knowing within me that all was well, and at the same time, I knew that somehow I needed to be present, perhaps just to be of comfort to her. And off we went. He was in complete organ shutdown and as she consulted with the doctors, they decided to take him into a sunroom before he was taken off the life support system. Almost as soon as they removed all the equipment that seemed to be keeping him alive, he began to rally. A miracle had occurred. As he gained strength, he was able to breathe on his own. Bringing kidney function back to normal required some dialysis treatments. Carol and I went into his room while this was going on and I nearly passed out. Never having met him, I recognized him immediately and I know he knew me as well. He looked at me with that same beautiful smile and then he winked. Carol saw it also and we both cried. He lived for seven years after everyone had given up. I guess I was a cooperative component for him and he was for me. I had my ideas of exactly the part I played in that scenario and couldn't wait to tell Jane and Rob all about it. It was wonderful to feel a part of something greater than anything I could ever imagine, and they thought so, too.

Channeling the Wisdom of a Tulip

The best channeling story from those early days that I can recall has never left me. It was springtime and I was meditating in my garden next to the brook that ran along our property line. I had planted tulips the year before and they were up; some had started to bloom as others were dropping their petals. The sun was warm on my face; I was relaxed and thought I was drifting off to sleep. Everything went fuzzy as I began to hear those flowers talking to me. I guess a part of me was wondering why these, my favorite flowers, didn't stay in bloom longer. They wanted me to understand, and then began their story: "The life is in the bulb, out of sight, and safe under the earth," they told me. "The flower is simply a joyous little show-off, but has the importance of carrying on the lineage, as do we." I listened for a long time as the devas of the tulips talked about the dormant power of multiplying themselves, the importance of the seasons and how they needed all the elements to bring life into being, and so on. I was an enraptured student listening to the wisdom of the flowers at the beginning of my channeling adventures. It was all very real and natural to me.

We are like tulips, requiring many cooperative components to fully bring our life into being.

While sitting on Jane's sofa on Water Street, watching her remove her glasses and lean forward in her chair as Seth began to talk, I remember the moment that I deliberately decided not to be a trance-channel. I simply didn't want to lose conscious time. I thought time was important and I did not understand the frequencies of consciousness. That was a choice point for me, and is as clear today as it was then. Instead of trance-channeling, I am a conscious channel. People have told me I am a natural teacher. I really attribute whatever abilities I have in that realm to my talent as a channel. I tune in and then can offer people assistance with what I receive. It is as simple as that. Channeling also makes my job as a teacher much easier because I can read the energy of the group and what their real needs of the day are. Then it is easier to take people where they want to go rather than where I think they should go, and everyone is happy. Of course I wanted to be a responsible channel and I went to great lengths to learn how to distinguish between subconscious channeling and clear channeling. Throughout the years, I have become quite good at deciphering clear channeling from the subconscious vanity or superiority types of channeling that used to be out there. I am aligned with universal knowledge and have the ability to access whatever is of interest to me at the time.

MY WAY SHOWERS

My religious orientation naturally tuned in to the familiar voices that I had come to respect and trust. I need to tell you that in my life I never really "bought" the full package religion thrusts upon us. However, I was and still am a very irreverent Reverend. The way I began to really accept Jesus was by seeing

Him as my older brother, someone who had been on this path before me, willing to guide me along and make my way easier.

Throughout the years as a pastor at my church in Las Vegas, and through my growing relationship, Jesus introduced me to many of the friends that He said guided Him. Those were sweet, innocent years for me that served to deepen my experience, awakening the Master Teacher within me. I understood Moses to be a mentor and teacher of Jesus. In meditation, I often visited their Ashram, which I believed to be in an impossible location to explain, but understood that it was within the Great Central Sun. I listened to them discuss the teachings that they were preparing, and I believed these to be plans to help humanity in this great time of awakening. When I was able to distance myself from the view I had been trained to believe about these wonderful souls, this allowed them to show me to myself. The teachings were profound. If I fell into the fear idea that I was not worthy of this interaction, I quickly lost the connection. Staying in the joy of the moment really held the vibration. Then it was imperative that I hold myself as an equal, with humility, to be teachable. This is a tricky area. It is necessary to be both gently joyous and teachable at the same time. One of the pitfalls is getting too cocky or having a big head, thinking you know more than others. You lose the connection and the Yabbits take over your education. I became highly aware of how my body reacted. I felt different "signals," such as an energy rush in my heart, or, when I was singing, my feet became so hot, I was not able to wear shoes. I learned to pay attention and focus on the subtleties of my thoughts and feelings so that I could stay clear and focused. During this time, one teaching that Jesus gave me that I continue to explore each day is, "I am in the world but not of it."

Through Esther Hicks, Abraham has reminded us that we are eternal beings. With that truth now solidly embodied in my mind, then I am Source energy and I continue to send a portion of myself into this physical life to see how far I can push the envelope, to explore how much self-realization I can align with while in this human body. On one episode of her show, Oprah Winfrey said, "We don't realize how powerful we are. It is like we are going around hiding in little human suits." Yes, we do wear human suits, and when I am done with this physical journey, I will then leave my suit behind and return to my Eternal Self. Eventually I will look for another avenue of exploration, as many have done before me, because once we understand who we really are, then the real fun begins.

So, I am in this world as a deliberate creator of reality—my own reality, to be specific. But I am not of this world and so anything goes, no limitations exist. I love my precious relationships with all the Great Teachers and Masters, and knowing our relationships will never end, I can have even more fun with them. I can realize that whether physical or non-physical, we are all learning and growing. We are all continually looking for love, and creative expression. We are all in this together!

I am in this world as a deliberate creator of reality. I am not of this world and so anything goes. No limitations exist.

The Masters Expand Also

Here is what I have been delighted to learn: our Master teachers, whether seen or unseen, are constantly expanding their consciousness also, often learning through us and alongside us. A person who channels is a cooperative component, a willing partner aligned to a certain frequency that allows the thoughts coming through to manifest into words and concepts that we can understand. Now we need new guidelines and new processes because there is more joy showing itself and a greater sense of self has been awakened. Plus, there is more recognition of the creative spirit within those around us, and a realization of the inherent brilliance in our young children. If you are a parent, think of how differently you are parenting today than perhaps you were parented growing up. I want you to be aware of how one generation begets the next and the next, how the expansion is occurring moment to moment.

Reading this book will open you to dormant ideas and unique thoughts just waiting to come forth just for you...just like the tulips waiting within their bulbs for the right season to bloom.

We are growing out of our limitations; it will serve us to have some new guidelines and processes to help us along. Better leverage for living a happier life.

Reflections

As you reflect on the words you just read, where did you pause? Which sentences made your heart quicken? Where are you in my stories? Use your journal, as thoughts vaporize and you might want to remember what you were thinking later on.

We are cooperative components for one another and the blessings are endless.

All of life is interconnected, and each of us has chosen a focus with which to discover the greatest within us. We have magnetized ourselves to others with a similar focus. Whether you call yourself a channel or intuitive, or do not subscribe to any of it, you are still part of the matrix of this stream of life and a vital component. It doesn't really matter what your belief system includes; what matters is that you believe in you! No matter what.

Chapter 12

Joy Alignment for Deliberate Creators

Enlightenment is a state of arrival: arriving, and arriving, and arriving.

We have covered so much already, including:

- ❧ A reconnection to your child-like essence of joy and enthusiasm.

- ❧ How the universal Laws of Attraction and Resonance affect your life experience.

- ❧ Learning from the chatter of your Yabbits.

- ❧ What happens to your creative abilities when you try to conform and become someone you are not and don't want to be.

- ❧ Using the powerful practices of basking, blessing, and goodness to shift into and sustain joy in your life.

- ❧ Gaining a new perspective on the creation of debt.

That is a lot of information to assimilate. I encourage you to reread some of the sections that piqued your interest, dog-ear the pages, highlight or underline sections, and contemplate on one line that calls out to you, especially when you need a joy boost. I promise that as your awareness expands, new pieces of information will bubble to the surface each time you read *Activate Joy*.

My desire is to help you gain the ability to reach and maintain a more consistent state of joy. In the beginning, having the information to know what you could do and actually doing it may seem worlds apart. Identifying the vibrational frequency you are in so you can know where you are in the moment will be helpful. To assist you even further, I developed the Joy Ruler. This tool serves as a gentle reminder to align with the greater part of us, that part that "knows our worth, knows our value, and knows our eternal nature."

From my experiences, I unified the teachings I have offered you to fit on this simple Joy Ruler. We humans love to compare and measure, so let's learn the art of measuring our alignment with Source and True Self.

For example, when I felt loss, I also felt hopelessness, which ultimately led to dis-pair. Now you will notice I deliberately spelled *dis-pair* differently to make a point. When we are that low on the ruler, we are "dis"ing everything: dis-carding, dis-assembling, dis-engaging in life. When I was low, I needed a reminder that "dis" equals separation, thus my dis-pair equaled separation from my joy and my spirit.

The Joy Ruler can help you determine where you are with the following:

> ❧ **Hope:** As you look at the Joy Ruler, notice that hope is central to the task. Hope is focused toward alignment with your true desires. Hope is the tipping point of the scale where you are thinking more about your dreams and what you want in life, rather

than what you lack. Hope must become more important than the "pity party" of lack so that you can make the shift into joy.

ᴔ **Doubt:** Doubting is a vibrational frequency that is very far from knowing. Doubt separates and cuts off. Doubt creates a gap that immobilizes our creative spirit. When in the process of mulling things over, there is a chronic voice of the doubting Yabbit that sends the message of mistrust—mistrusting the universe, mistrusting others, and more importantly, mistrusting yourself. If you find yourself stuck in this type of mulling, use the Basking Process or Goodness Process to help shift your point of attraction.

Through years of healing and expanded awareness, I have learned that doubt seems to be the major Yabbit that carries the power to turn our heads away from our dreams. Enough doubt will successfully limit joy to the point that you can become numb to it. You know that place where just hearing laughter and happy people talking makes you mad? I've always been a bottom-line person, so I am focusing on the insidious aspect of doubt to help us gain further clarity on the acceptance of knowing worthiness.

ᴔ **Rage:** I have depicted a type of rage that is "white rage" on this ruler because this is the more non-violent form. As I work with people, I find that rage, and feelings associated with rage, are not really at the front of the problem for most. Rage and anger seem to be a reaction when one feels powerless to get what is wanted, and for most, real rage is often short-lived. A great teacher of mine, Bashar, once told us that rage was a good thing for 30 seconds because it was a powerful indicator of what you do not want. Okay, and now what? How do I get what I want? According to the newest teachings of Abraham-Hicks, "Turn in the direction of what you do want and control what you can control, your feelings." When you look at the Joy Ruler, it looks happy. Moving out of rage requires a focus of hope. Focus on something good in your life; focus on something you can control—how you feel.

ஒ **Despair:** We are not really equipped to stay in rage for long periods of time. When we allow ourselves to stay dis-empowered through chronic negative thinking, and because we didn't get what we wanted, the impotent raging retreats into despair. Despair then imprisons and shackles us in its dungeon of hopelessness.

ஒ **Hopelessness:** Without a deliberate choice here, it is challenging to find a way to empower yourself back into some sense of joy when numbness and depression set in. It's interesting to me, however, that with the many people I have worked with intimately in my capacity as teacher/healer, even those in deep depression will tell me about moments in their day when they feel good or have some creative thoughts come to them. To get from hopeless to hope requires awareness so you can tap into joy during the times that you actually do feel good.

    ✿ **True Self/Source/Soul:** When people try to describe our our "it," they use these three terms to express the same thing. The term is not as important as the concept. If, somehow, we can accept that we are eternal beings living in a human body for a short time, and living over and over again, perhaps we can allow ourselves to understand how this eternal part of us, our soul, could continually send us signals, like beacons of light calling us home, back to our True Self. By establishing a healthy connection to our True Self/Source/Soul, we are constantly reminded of our birthright.

There is nothing like having a simple reminder that you can have in your pocket or purse that will remind you to bask in the joy of living. Use the ruler to lift your heart when you feel stuck. Focus on some of uplifting words such as *luscious*, *delightful*, and *splendid* as your imagination takes you on a joy ride. In this way, you will discover how easy it can be to reconnect to your soul, inner self, the greater part of you. Be careful though; activating joy is contagious.

Meet Joe

In 1994, a couple from Jacksonville, Florida, attended my first healing school faithfully for four years. The husband (Joe) always looked happy and put together. He participated in all the processes and on the outside seemed to be just fine. At the class before graduation, his wife came to me for help. It seemed that Joe was deeply depressed. He had been out of work for some time. He would go home after each class and get into bed and not come out. They had a son who was 5 years old, but

Joe was deep in depression that he could not work through and was not available to be a dad or much of a husband. I am an energy healer, not a clinician, and am very cautious about dealing with what seems to be in a psychiatrist's or psychologist's domain; however, because Joe was my student and would soon graduate, I agreed to talk to him about how he was handling his emotional issues.

Perhaps this is the perfect story to illustrate how our eternal natures communicate. Before every session I always do my prayers, blessings, and clearings; it is just standard procedure. In this process, I align my soul or higher-self energies with my clients' soul or higher-self consciousnesses. My focus is completely centered on, in this case, Joe and his highest good. This allows a channel, or a corridor of light, to open that flows both ways, soul to soul, from Joe to me and from me to Joe.

These are live sessions either sitting person to person or on the phone. In this case, I began by simply asking him how he felt. As he described the heavy feelings weighing him down, I began to get visual impressions of a wet blanket covering him from head to toe. Without any prompting on my part, Joe soon began to describe this wet blanket that seemed to continually get heavier and heavier. With that statement, I knew our soul connection was in sync and just allowed the process to reveal itself. I asked him how he could breathe; that made him laugh and he said he didn't know. It felt to me as if he (his Higher Self or Soul) took over the reins in that moment and I simply moved with the currents of knowledge and wisdom guiding him back into control of his life. It wasn't long before the wet blanket dissolved into a light, summer-weight little throw. Then, in another phone session, the energy of his son came in and removed it, then climbed into bed with him.

Joe was a changed man. It took nine sessions to allow the layers of suffocation to resolve. I credit this miraculous (some would say) healing to a combination of elements. First, Joe had been coming to the school for four years and had completed many homework-healing sessions. He had a working understanding of his own Higher Self and Soul nature. And most importantly, he wanted to live again.

Just a very short time after we finished working together in distance sessions specifically for the depression, Joe decided he would go back to work. This occurred during a period of two months because he found a reason to hope for a better life.

Although I did not have the Joy Ruler when I worked with Joe, I can clearly see what led him out of dis-pair. Once he was able to access hope, this aligned him with his true self and the joy in his life. He began to feel better and better about himself and his family, and his depression lifted, which aligned him with the Source of his Being who only knows abundance and well-being.

Meet Angie

I am very close to my friend Angie who has been held captive in the jaws of despair, gloom, and doom. She is a young girl who has come to the brink of death several times in car accidents, or with illness in hospitals. In 2010, she was bitten by a brown recluse spider and battled with the horrible flesh-eating venom. Getting her in the vicinity of hope had been near impossible. I decided to give it another try. Perhaps if I could somehow help Angie find some hope for her life, it could wake her up. These sessions were all done in person, using the same techniques I described with Joe. Inspired, I asked her to hold the little Joy Ruler, and look at where she thought she was on the scale at that moment. We discussed each of the life-threatening experiences she had been through. Even though she kept on facing death, it didn't seem that it was her time. Death kept spitting her back into life. And suddenly, we looked at the gaping hole in her leg, and actually began to laugh as we talked about how it felt to be eaten alive. Then, Angie shifted from looking at the hole to looking at her life from a larger vantage point. In that moment she had an *ah-ha!* and realized she wasn't meant to die so young. Angie experienced a self-realization about her belief of thinking that others would save her. Without any faith in herself she could not access hope, and, with no hope in her mind, she would be destined to continue cycling in and out of nowhere. With this self-realization, Angie's faith in herself shifted and she naturally moved into alignment. Today she has found herself, has a wonderful job, and is beginning to live her life as she always dreamed would be possible.

How You Can Use the Joy Ruler

If you find yourself on the down side of the scale, imagine yourself looking at a rainbow and remember the promise of your birthright: joy. Choose to be a deliberate creator of the reality you want by focusing on and appreciating where you are. Then see the bright sunlight of hope smiling at you and acknowledge that happy feeling beginning to arise within your heart that wants to expand. See that ball sitting over the "b" in doubt? That ball is there to remind you to find a way to bounce into alignment with the highest in you. The way you bounce is to think better-feeling thoughts, look for anything that will help you smile, watch a cartoon.

COUNTERACTING RESISTANCE

Sometimes when I talk to people about joy, the resistance is so strong you can feel it; they might even take a step back away from me. On the Joy Ruler you could say that resistance is on the other side of hope, and often the person is in the thick muck of doubt. When I feel into this particular resistant energy, it is similar to unyielding cables, or thick bungee cords that have been fortified during years of accepted certainties that we have accepted as facts. From those entrained to believe life is hard, I hear their Yabbits chime in and say, "I don't have what it takes. If I looked different, if I was smarter...you should see what it's like out there." Resistance is simply a consistent focus on what you don't have.

I have two rules of empowerment to counteract the effect of resistance:

1. Never push, just offer this statement: "If you could have anything right now, what would make you happy?" This statement is magical, throws the Yabbits off-guard, and brings you directly in line with what you want.

2. Always hold the vision of hope, recognizing that joy is what we are all made of. Do your best not to enter into any discussion on the negative side of the fence. It takes some practice, but through the years, my students and I have gotten pretty good at it. The old technique of mirroring positive statements helps to reflect hope. Active listening is part of this technique. The challenge is to stay aligned yourself, and if others really want to stay in their resistance, let them, and come back later. You can't fix others; only they can discover the path within themselves.

SPACE TO GROW

It is so important to offer others the space to walk their own path and keep your judgments about what you think they should be doing out of it. One simple thought I could offer here is to never say anything that smacks of advice or that would seem to take away free choice. This is a form of coercion and it always backfires, sometimes by making the resistance even stronger.

Let me give you some ideas of how you can hold a positive and empowering space for others, for yourself, and for the world at large:

- **Know that joy and unconditional love are the very essence of life.** Let's take the resistant thought and offer a blessing into the resistance. When we bless something, we are aligning with the positive intent behind the resistance, and then acknowledging that, because of the resistance, we grew and learned how to bounce into a positive and more loving response.

- **Realize any cords of attachment you feel are not real,** and dissolve them in your mind's eye. Cords of attachment go both ways, creating debt that can never be paid off. You can be corded to another through guilt, which is really the big one. Vice versa, you may have sent a cord of attachment into someone by guilting that person into doing something he or she really doesn't want to do. Bouncing and alignment are the antidotes you are looking for—fast, easy, and immediate.

- ❧ **Never agree with the false premise of resistance.**
  It doesn't feel good. It is only the Yabbits talking.

- ❧ **Realize there is a gap to be closed** on the bridge
  to the freedom to experience joy, and begin to see
  that gap closing. Notice how good that feels.

- ❧ **Work on building faith and feeling good.** Using
  the Goodness Process is one way to build faith and
  dissolve separation.

So here it is…hold on to hope as you ride the wave of faith,
feeling good because you know that you are goodness, and joy
is just waiting to tickle your fancy.

PRACTICE THE POWER OF KNOWING

In learning how to use the Joy Ruler and learning how to
bounce into alignment, you are strengthening your knowing,
which is a key element in holding the energy of joy longer and
longer. Knowing is an intangible essence; no one can teach you
how to know, it just naturally happens as you allow yourself to
focus on joy.

In knowing, there is a sense of confidence and well-being.
Questions you might have will lead to the next level of knowing.
As a minister, I have always been curious about the idea of
enlightenment. I had a feeling that enlightenment is really a
perception of where we are in relation to…what? Our teachers
from the East have given us many ideas of what enlightenment
is, and I was looking for clarity on the subject. I am an or-
dinary woman who has had extraordinary experiences…I can
feel enlightened about one thing and not about another; I can

perform a miracle one day and not the next. What is enlightenment, anyway? This question rolled around in my mind for years without any real satisfaction.

Then one day in meditation, I felt the presence of the great Buddha. Quite innocently, I asked him to teach me about enlightenment.

"What is enlightenment?" I asked.

He replied, "Enlightenment is a state of arrival: arriving, and arriving, and arriving."

The visual impression I received was riding on a train, going from station to station, getting off the train and spending time doing whatever it is you came to do, and then getting back on the train once more.

"The point is the thrill of the ride," Buddha said.

This was a profound teaching for me because, through his transmission of a great truth, I began to realize the power of our infinite creative nature. There is a deep knowing about enlightenment within me now that cannot be shaken. This is my knowing. If someone wants to know what I know, I'll tell them, and then I let it go without any need to convince them. When we arrive at knowing, an unfathomable feeling of well-being washes over our entire self. We become confident, we trust ourselves, and the need to argue our point to make others agree with us dissolves. The false need to make someone else believe "whatever" becomes irrelevant. Alignment with your inner being has occurred, which naturally brings forth an outlook from the vantage point of confidence. The kaleidoscope turns and your perspective changes.

Knowing your birthright of worthiness, goodness, and joy allows power and leverage in every choice you make. As soon as you know, another level of knowing has been born and begs to also be known; this is in essence the infinite creative process. If we make a choice, you and I, here and now, to accept this as the fundamental principle with which we entered this life experience, the knowing of it will come forth. Alignment becomes evident. The evidence is joy.

ALIGNING WITH FAITH AND WORTHINESS

Rulers help us to draw straight lines and measure how far we need to go to reach a certain point. The points are indicators of where we are, or where we think we are. Hope is the center point on the Joy Ruler. Hope will open your awareness to faith, faith in the things you have dreamed of and not yet seen. Most of all, hope opens you to faith in yourself and your magnificent creative nature. Faith is the belief that what you desire will happen even though the evidence of it has not yet appeared. Faith honored awakens joy, which beckons you into its vortex of freedom and happiness. When you are at the point of hope, you can easily move into basking and be able to shift away from despair and separation.

A great deal of our lives can be spent in torture, unsure of where we stand in relation to worthiness. Religion plays a big part in the trap of worthiness versus unworthiness, and the gap between our True Self and the personality self is wide for some. Gosh, we have judged ourselves harshly, on spirituality, intelligence, body shape, artistic abilities, just plain ability, financial standing, and speech. Comparison has been the measuring stick, creating expectation and then attracting our comparable reality, and for the most part we have unknowingly allowed the Yabbits controlling interest. What do the Yabbits say and how much influence do their voices have in your life? Those Yabbits are the traps and signs. They are showing you where you are disconnected or vulnerable, where you can make a change.

Is God outside us or within us? If God is within us, just how far in? Is God better than we are? Is God greater than we are? Most of us have been trained to believe that we are not worthy of that which we deem greater than we are, and for some, that belief is a pretty wide gap to bridge. For a long time, New Age teachings have told us we are God, we are Source. And boy, have the Yabbits said a lot about that idea. Watch how entrained we have become to seeing ourselves as small and insignificant, unworthy to the point that we expect and anticipate limitation, and in doing this have created a limiting experience. We expect to have to work hard, suffer, and toil for our bread. In the past we have expected too little for ourselves, and now it is time to stop and smell the roses. Rise up, reawaken, and allow joy to be heard.

Joy is the secret DNA: Divine Natural Allowing

Jesus, my teacher and friend, in His most poignant moment, told us, "Greater things than these shall you do." In all the years working with Him, He has always made me feel His equal. He is often my conscience, constantly reminding me how great I am, my encourager, and my champion, picking me up until I could walk on my own. Then He runs alongside me, sweetly enjoying the wind on His face and the sand beneath His feet.

So what do you say to get in alignment? Repeat the following statements enthusiastically and out loud:

I am a worthy, deserving person.

I am worthy of happiness.

I am worthy of thinking my own thoughts.

I am worthy of feeling my own feelings.

I am worthy of loving and being loved.

I am worthy of living my fortune; it is my birthright.

I am worthy of being at peace with myself and the world.

I have complete faith in myself, and I know my worthiness.

JOY RULES!

The purpose of the Joy Ruler is to keep reminding us that joy rules and we are all superstars, great, renowned bridge builders closing that gap, creating a new pathway of alignment with joy and happiness. The more of us who choose to follow that pathway, the easier it will become. The time is now. This is our time to come into alignment with all that we have asked for and all that we want. This is what I have dedicated my life to, and now I see that the final pieces of the puzzle, at least for this phase of my life, are magnetically being drawn into place.

Right now, as I write this book, it is late summer of 2010. What seems like the eighth wonder of the world to me is being completed—a spectacular bridge that spans the Hoover Dam and the Colorado River connecting Nevada and Arizona. I have watched this gargantuan undertaking and the revealing correlation to our own reaching during the past several years.

Closing the gap in the Hoover Dam Bridge

With every healing comes another ray of inspiration, another ray of hope for who we are and why we are here. Look at the photo of the bridge. The massive gap is now closed and in the final stages of completion. With the mountains in the background, the bridge becomes a rainbow of promise spanning the years from 1936 to today. As we allow our joy to be more and more important in our everyday lives, reaching that promise we made to ourselves before we were born is fulfilled. Each day, just like the bridge, our life continues to expand into greater fulfillment. We know it now beyond a sliver of doubt.

The gap is closed

Through the years I have watched hundreds of my students free themselves from the burdens of fear, terror, and disgust. Little by little, they grab onto those rays of light and lift themselves into a place where they can really believe in themselves, and their value in life. I am a testimony to this happening in my own life as well.

The powerful pull of alignment asks us to have more faith in our perpetual and eternal nature. The bridge we are building is a bridge of faith reinforced by joy. Faith in our worthiness that is strong enough and powerful enough to bring us into the knowing of it. To believe in the joy of our worthiness is no longer good enough. We must believe in it enough to live it enthusiastically.

To know worthiness is a key to consistently experiencing the activation of joy in your life…and being able to sustain it.

The Bridge at the Hoover Dam is now complete

CHAPTER 13

JOY IS YOU!
YOU ARE THE
MAGNIFICENT PEARL

WE ARE CONSTANTLY BEING CALLED INTO JOY BY
THE SOURCE WITHIN US. A NEVER-ENDING STREAM
OF LIGHT THAT SHINES BRIGHTLY, LEADING US INTO
THE VORTEX OF OUR MAGNIFICENT SELF, TO BASK IN
THE REALIZATION OF THE DIVINE SELF THAT WE HAVE
ALWAYS BEEN.

A pearl begins as a tiny grain of sand that, with time, is smoothed into a jewel of great value. This transformation occurs within the jagged shells of oysters. The priceless pearl appears hidden inside this mollusk with strength and skill required to open its vortex of beauty. Her fortune so generously formed from what originated as a pure tone, with provocation for great wealth and magnificence, is ready now to be claimed.

Revealing the "mystery of you" is the same process. You and I are the pearl of great price; we are the unique, one-of-a-kind, lustrous beauty that wants to be free from our self-imposed (s)hell. We want to be seen and known, touched and loved. We are our own fortune. Just take a moment and breathe that in, realize the infinite magnitude of these few words, and then tune in and feel the impact within you before you read on.

Each of us has been trained by our surroundings to develop a false reality. If we were oysters, our outer ego would be seen as a shell that has been encrusted with demanding parasites or barnacles during our lifetime. Oysters and their barnacles are stationary beings. They find one safe place and stay there for life, all in the relentless pursuit of nothing, unless of course a storm blows them out of their comfort zone. Some realization!

We now have the knowledge of freedom from limitation, and the wisdom to apply that knowledge in our everyday lives. We no longer have to wait for a storm to brew and then blow us out of our comfort zones. There is no longer any reason to put up with demanding, parasitic Yabbits that run and ruin our day. And most of all…there is no reason to hide your magnificence. Feel the exhilaration of reaching into the moment and lifting your lustrous pearl up for the world to see. Notice the way your heart flutters when you even think that could be so, and then the "Oh yah, it's time." The Source within you, the greater part of you that can never be separated from you, celebrates that realization. Bravo!

I love nature. I love everything about the natural world that we are privileged to live in. Many years ago, when I first began my spiritual journey, I watched a National Geographic program about the seals that gather on the Galapagos Islands. I always realize something wonderful when I watch nature shows, and that night I listened intently as I learned more about the natural order of wildlife. What stayed with me for years is an experience I had that evening. The narrator spoke about how a mother seal could always find her pup. A sound frequency is unique, like a fingerprint, to all forms of life, and that sound is also like a beacon of connective consciousness. The mother always finds her pup because she knows how to hone in on the frequency emitted through the light body of her pup over all the other sounds being emitted on the noisy beach. That evening, during the program, I heard this whispered in my ear: "I am always with you, through the tone that brought you forth, I am always connected with you, I can always find you, and you can always connect with me." Later I wrote a small booklet called the "Tone of the God Self," which anchored that teaching, and served me continually in all the days that have followed. There is a great relief that happens within the core of our being, knowing that we are not lost, we are always enfolded within the arms of love that are the essence of who we are on every level. There is nowhere love is not.

There is a great relief that happens within the core of our being, knowing that we are not lost, we are always enfolded within the arms of love that are the essence of who we are on every level.

We are constantly being called into joy by the Source within us, a never-ending stream of light that shines brightly, leading us into the vortex of our magnificent self, to bask in the realization of the Divine Self that we have always been. I'm sure you have heard it said before that we are Spirit having a physical experience. In other words, the greater part of who we are, beyond human bodies, is our soul or spirit. Our soul or spirit resides inside our body as our individual consciousness, which has entered into this reality to experience physical life. This means that, at the core, beyond our physical bodies, we are an eternal being. The eternal being that you are existed before your body, and will continue to exist after your death. Our eternal being has an opportunity to experience being human with all the wonder that goes along with this. The physical aspect we live right now is only a fraction of our Source energy that is available to us. And most importantly, that Source energy is the reality of who we are. I wondered, what's holding us back? Why aren't all of us living the amazing life we know is available? How have we missed the various "Greater than this shall you do" teachings that have been given to us by *all* the Masters?

The Source within me gave me answers through the many teachers who have empowered my life. Let me share some of these ideas with you.

"What you put out you get back."—Bashar, *Blueprint for Life*

"Ask and it is given."—Abraham, Law of Attraction

"You create your own reality."—Seth, *Seth Speaks*

"Be happy."—Buddha

"You reap what you sow."—Galatians 6:7

"I am in the world but not of it."—Jesus

Alchemy is the act of transforming Yabbits into valuable jewels.

So how does this work, exactly? Through free choice. Here is the simplicity of it all:

There is no great force making the choices for you.

There is nothing to live up to.

There is nowhere to go.

Every moment is perfect and complete in of itself.

You will always want more so choose what you want.

Heaven or hell is created through your choices.

Everything is good and very good.

It is through choice, or what some call our free will, that we decide which layer will be more lustrous for us in the moment; on one side we bless, on the other we condemn. There is no center place, no sitting on the fence, no so-called halfway house. As we go through our life sifting through the sands of experience, we either bless or condemn everything we encounter. Think about it: Even the smallest detail has a magnetic pull, pulling us toward what we want and pulling us toward what we don't want as well. That's an important idea to grasp. When we condemn something, the energy around us calcifies and becomes hard against the world. When we make a habit of condemning, we set in motion the frequency of the Law of Resonance that summons the Law of Attraction. Similar thoughts are continually attracted and hitch a ride like parasitic barnacles. Left to simmer long enough, these guys can weigh heavily in our life experience, holding our shell tightly closed and unyielding, creating a deluge of Yabbits that wait for us to transform them into valuable jewels.

Deliberate Creators
Deliberately Choose

Deliberate creators deliberately choose what they want. Once you have knowledge, and the awareness of the impact of your thoughts, you have the advantage. Deliberate creators understand the polarity of choice and deliberately choose what feels better. The radiant pearl of joy is the indicator. Let's move to the next level of this teaching. One of the many choices presented to us throughout our lives is to conform. Some of us have been erroneously taught that to be loved we need to conform to whatever so that we may receive love. Even though conformity goes against all of our natural guidance of uniqueness, we learned to conform, because the need to be safe, to be loved, to belong, to feel connected, to survive, to find power, was stronger.

Using a Dr. Philism, "How's that working for you?" Probably not very well, because conforming contracts and defies the natural order of flow, and also makes us uncomfortable. We know that conformity on so many levels is like a death sentence to our creative nature, in that conforming disconnects us from the very things we long to be, do, and have. Remember how angry it made you when you did what someone else wanted you to and you had another definite idea in mind? You were thinking, "Okay, but I won't like it." Or, "Okay, you're right, I'm wrong." Disempowerment upsets our balance, throwing us off course. When we lose the ability to use joy in our expression, especially in our formative young years, when or if we begin to look to others for validation, to tell us how we are doing. We become rebellious, demanding our own way; maybe we get our way and maybe we are shot down. Anger erupts, and the only relief from anger often comes from condemning yourself or others. You are playing the blame game, making others wrong so you can feel good about yourself. And the Yabbit of negative self-esteem takes control. Can you see how we continue to hold the course of condemning for the sheer relief we think it brings us? And surely as you navigate the Yabbit world, there is a type of relief, blowing off steam really, that occurs. Now let's learn how to steer our yacht into calmer and more beautiful waters.

THE POWER OF DELIBERATE BLESSING

Earlier in *Activate Joy*, we spent a special time exploring a whole chapter on the Art of Blessing. Now let's go deeper into this teaching.

I had a powerful opportunity to use deliberate blessing. I was in my kitchen with a good friend having a wonderful conversation over a cup of coffee. She reminded me of something I needed to take a look at and change. I didn't realize how hurtful her words were, until I was triggered by an unpleasant call I received while we were talking. Not long after that, another aggravating event was in my face. I was out of my happiness vortex and in reaction mode, drawing more challenges to me. While experiencing emotional overwhelm, I was in reaction/protection mode because I lost sight of my joy, and in that moment, the fight-or-flight mechanism of survival was unleashed within me. I was angry, which showed me what I absolutely do not want in my experience. We were getting ready to meet my friend's daughter and son-in-law for lunch, and now the happy mood we had been in was gone. Out of alignment with who I really am, I was reacting instinctively to the unpleasant feelings, which felt awful. Going back to the point where the chaos began a short 20 minutes earlier, my friend and I were both seeing the same issue through our own projections and perceptions. Unable to gain any satisfaction or control the outcome of the conversation, and realizing this was a great opportunity presented to us simultaneously, we both began to bounce back to our preferred experience. I said first, "This is not the way I want to spend our time together."

She said, "Me neither." I went into speaking my blessing and appreciating everything about her I could think of for some time, then she did the same for me. By the time we got to our destination, we were both free of the anger that had us both in its grip. Friends and colleagues for many years, there was no way we didn't know what was going on. It still wasn't easy because there is that righteous Yabbit that wants to win...

THE PARADIGM SHIFT: CREATING NEW STRATEGIES FOR DELIBERATE CONSCIOUS CREATORS

Earlier I wrote that the key to living the paradigm shift is practicing unconditional love. I heard it said once that it is very easy for a monk in a cave to practice love because there is no need to interact with others. Once you finish the last page of this book, you will go out into the world and interact with other people. Some will be happy and uplifting, others will be suffering. Running away and hiding from people who are in pain or are experiencing a rough spot is not the answer; instead, learn to be present with them without falling into the same "pit." Remember, "You are in the world, but not of it." Keep your eye on you first and realize relationships will always play an important role in our lives. Here are two examples for you to consider:

Example 1: How do I stay centered in my own thoughts and feelings and true to myself when someone else needs to tell me about their pain?

In January 2011, while on a cruise in New Zealand and Australia, I completed this book. At that time devastating rains and floods occurred in Queensland. People lost homes and some lost their lives. I was at lunch with two Australian ladies who were justifiably worried about their families and the flooding of their towns and cities. One of the easy traps to fall into is looking into *your* experience to see what *they* are feeling. The minute you open a sympathetic resonance with what another person is going through, you are out of your center. As I listened to their worries, I deliberately practiced staying centered in a blessing consciousness which allowed me to also be very aware. I cared about my new friends, I cared about the panic in the hearts of all the people in Australia, and I recognized we are all one. Knowing this, my intention was to help relieve their tension without breaking the unconditional loving energy I had already established. This skill I will give you I learned many years ago and have always taught in the Inner Focus School. The basic principles rest in Sound Healing. I will give you a simple guideline to work with, and once you try it, you will see how often you have done this very thing.

Accept the fact that you have the capacity to lift consciousness without taking anything away from yourself in the process. You are a vibrational being who is eternal in nature; therefore, vibration and sound are inherent in your core consciousness.

As we began lunch, my friends had just called home for the latest updates. The news was less than hopeful and so they were both on the downside of the emotional scale. I purposely did not enter into the conversation, yet continued to listen with half an ear, not listening to the details, but the sound of eternal beings struggling in the moment, while having my lunch at the same time. When people are relating a dramatic story, their voices will pinpoint the real fears with the rise and fall of their voices within the sounds of the story. Instead of listening to every detail of the situation, I listened for the cues in the rise and fall of their voices. When someone is telling you about an emotionally charged experience, the sounds from his or her voice are like a song that has high peaks and low points, a chorus, and the song will end with the final note at a low tone or sigh. Knowing that, I became conscious of when the first few emotional stanzas were ready to leave the "discordant tones" and resolve themselves. You want to listen to someone with half an ear as he or she is going through this process, and then, when he or she arrives at that point of resolve, it might feel like a lull in the conversation. With my Australian friends, they both began to eat a little of their lunch.

The sounds of the resolve are the tones you want to focus on, and then something will come to you that you can talk about or do to lift the energy. So as that time came, matching the tonal quality of my voice to their last melody, I began in very soft tones to tell them about a wonderful adventure I had the day before in Tasmania. As I talked about my adventure, in a boat in a turbulent sea with rain and low-lying clouds, I was calling them into my more relaxed frequency and they were able to feel immediate relief from their stress. Seeing their interest peek through, I continued to relay how it seemed to me that a Star Trek adventure could have been filmed that day, and on and on until we were all smiling and talking about other things.

Two things were served:

1. I did not need to enter their pain (or world of pain) to be *with* them.

2. Unconditional love cared enough about my friends to respectfully bring some relief and provide a space for all of us to be in the vortex of centeredness and genuine caring together, which allowed a spiraling of energy to occur. Now, the next time they approach the subject, and because joy has been activated, it will be from that higher vantage point we had all previously reached. Of course, this is also true for you as continued practice allows for trust in yourself to take hold.

Often, when we are learning something new, such as, "you create your own reality," we might be tempted to use harsh language to protect the fragile barriers we have carefully constructed for ourselves. "You create your own reality" can be used as a bludgeoning tool condemning something that is clearly out of another's control. Unconditional love does not scratch, tear, bully, or knock down.

Unconditional love does not look for outcomes. Unconditional love is allowing and always seeking to be uplifted.

Example #2: Holding your center when a relationship is completing.

Because we are first and foremost vibrational beings, we are people who *feel* deeply. All relationships are meant for expansion and growth, no matter what they may look like. We also must realize that because we are all eternal beings, it probably is not the first time we have encountered this person or persons. That being said, this can apply to personal relationships or job-related relationships. *The key is hidden in how we relate in the relationship now.*

My example is one of a three-year relationship with someone I cared for deeply. There were countless times when we were inseparable, along with times when we had other things to do and our time together was less important. Whether a relationship is long-term or short-lived, this a universal example. The first two years of this relationship were fabulous, joyous, and exciting. We experienced the force of a very deep love for one another. When the New Year came, there was a shift in our relationship. My friend had made a decision for himself, which was more of an ultimatum delivered in a loving and caring way to me. Realizing that I thought I wanted a different outcome from our relationship, it put me at a choice point.

To give the cycle of a relationship a more universal context, let's look at the power of the tides in the Earth's oceans for an illustration of the tidal force behind relationships. The oceans have been here since the beginning of time and they accurately represent the power behind all relationships. First there is the inflow of energy, the inspiration that attracts the relationship to begin with. Second, the ebbing begins; the sea reverses the flow of energy. Both must occur for the power to build and expand the present energies. There is also a third phase called the neap, a very brief time of rest that happens twice a month as the tide turns. To give you an even better example, it is like the breath. There is an inflow of breath, then a second or two when the breath turns to the outflow of breath.

I love the idea of using the tides in this illustration for relationship, because of the emotional nature of relationships. We go through a wide range of emotions as we relate to one another. One might say that we ride the tides. There are assumptions, projections, expectations, and adaptations that flow in and out of any given moment. Relationships are perhaps the most volatile of cooperative components we can focus on to understand where we are. As a relationship is winding down, you may have noticed that it sometimes takes a while for that completion to manifest.

For me it took a year of *slowly* getting a handle on what I wanted, because I didn't know. I went back to my teachings from Bashar, the telepathic beings from our *now* future. Here is what they had to say: "Allow us to remind you that we always allow any relationship any individuals find themselves attracted into to be an obvious reflection of the things they need to understand and learn at that point. And we allow the relationship to be what it is for, rather than what we *think* it should be. We do not put expectations on them for what we think they ought to be. We know they are there to serve us; we know we are there to serve them, and we rejoice in the spontaneous co-creation." In the past, we have been taught that we need reasons, a "something" that occurred so that we have permission to leave the relationship. The condemning aspect comes in when that someone else does something seemingly wrong to you. The good news is that we *do not need to feel devastated when a relationship ends.* We have advanced in consciousness and no longer operate under the rules of the old paradigm. When it is time to end a relationship, you can accomplish this with grace, dignity, goodness, and blessing.

My friend and I spent the rest of that year gently distancing from one another. There was a move to another town, less frequent calls and get-togethers, until near the end of that year it felt like we were both futilely trying to stop the ebbing tide. I felt like I was holding my breath with lungs about to burst, not wanting to be the one to let go. This year was also the time of some of the greatest spiritual growth I had experienced so far; I was writing this book, accepting myself in a more satisfying way, and realizing the choice to ebb the relationship had already been made. Because we are emotional beings, the signs were always present: the discomfort, the hesitation, the procrastination. I also realized that the debt that I was incurring was mounting up because I was not willing to follow my heart and gracefully move on by completing this relationship. Now we are learning to become more aware more quickly, thus healing the wounds of the past and moving on when that is what is wanted, *without blame and drama.*

I remember asking Bashar once when Darryl was visiting in my home, "How long are you usually in relationship?" The answer is a constant reminder of just how far our society needs to come. "We are with someone until we are not." Isn't that great?

So this is the part I really want to convey:

When the moment comes and a relationship is ending, how do you hold your center as the words are finally being said? Use the Goodness Process and the blessing tools.

You already know the energy is moving in that direction, so make sure that you are in a space of love and light. You do that by blessing and seeing the highest and best in your partner. Breathe easily and bless the movement and expansion that is coming into your lives. Next, accept the blessing of the freedom that is about to happen for both of you. Realize joy activated is freedom.

Bask in the beautiful memories. After the closing statements have been made, take time to bask in memories of the best that your relationship offered to both of you. Spend time focused on the poignant moments as well as the funny ones. Appreciate and honor one another for all that has been brought into your lives because of your relationship.

Deliberately set the resonance frequency. Remember that how you are *feeling* will create a similar resonance frequency that naturally activates the Law of Attraction. If you feel empty, you open up the resonance to the feeling of devastation. If you shift your focus until you feel appreciation, you will attract more to appreciate. Now, appreciate that having done this, you will leave this relationship whole, complete, and eager as you look forward into your expanding future. So often, because this information is not really understood, we tend to leave relationships shattered and in pain. Activating joy eliminates the need for that step. As my friend and I parted, there was a relief on both of our parts that was almost explosive. Activating joy allows freedom in all arenas because there is nothing to hold onto but the forward movement of joy.

GETTING TO JOY

There is leverage in seeing things from a new perspective, but how can you get there? Know that whatever "it" is, when you are unable to bless a thing in the moment, try to feel into the discomfort, and allow your awareness to move with the energy of condemning. Where do you go? Whatever you are judging outside of yourself, I promise will always lead back to you. So it is important to spend just a minute clarifying where this energy lives inside of you.

Feel into the depth of the thing you are condemning, notice which way you are facing, and then deliberately physically turn your hands and head in the opposite direction. This action is a signal to your body stating that you are aware and ready to follow your natural emotional instinct. Very soon, joy will begin to peek out from under the covers and bubble to the surface of your consciousness. Deliberately and sincerely begin to bless and appreciate you for turning your attention to what you really want in your life experience. Stay with yourself right now. Feel into the idea of blessing. Don't skip ahead and try to bless the thing you are condemning just yet; begin to flow with the feeling of the self-blessing.

Now, self-mastery comes in. Negative emotions are gushing out everywhere when the plug has been pulled and you can recognize that you are out of control. As soon as you can, *stop!* Emotions flow in cycles and the mastery is to seize the moment and stop the emotion. Feel into the blessing, feel into your lustrous pearl, the beauty that you are. Stay conscious, reach into the soft folds of that oyster until you are able to lift your pearl easily into the light. Now, you can deliberately make a new choice.

Here is an example of how to deliberately make a new, focused choice:

I am blessed with a good life, I am blessed. My dog is blessed with a good life, my dog is blessed. My park is blessed with a good life. I love walking my dog in that park and feeling carefree. Love is everywhere, it is in my family, it is in my government, it is in the friends I have gathered around me. Love is in the water I drink and the love I seek is always there waiting for me...

...and so on for a few more sentences until you can feel easy and caught up in the beauty of the moment. See if you can send a blessing to the thing you were condemning. If not, go back to something easier, and then keep coming back to the pearl that is forming within that hardened shell that was determined not to allow you to open it up. Be patient, allowing your new awareness to unfold. Just open to the goodness in all things.

Those pesky Yabbits are just waiting for the opportunity to get your attention. Your power is realized as you shift gears from reactive choice to deliberate choice. Use the following focus statements to live your awareness:

- **Focus on joy:** Make this exercise fun.

- **Focus on ease and flow:** There is nothing in your way.

- **Focus on happiness:** Feel the effervescent happiness bubbles.

- **Focus on blessing and appreciating everything:** Look, see, and appreciate everything around you, lifting away the idea of burdens, any resistance...

Deliberate choice is about self-centered focus, which allows you to find joy presenting itself within the thing that you are condemning, and ultimately find it within you. This transforms everything.

Okay, now that might work for some things, but soon there will be what I call a "toe tripper." Then you will say, "Oh, there is *no* way I can bless that." As you are confronted with judgments, and condemnation of a situation, person, or persons, here is what you do: Feel the vibrational frequency of what you are condemning. This is the true meaning of "turn the other cheek." If you catch yourself condemning, stop. Now decide where you want to go. What is the result you are really looking for in your heart? I imagine you want more good feelings, so choose something that gives you good feelings. Turn all of your focus and attention on that place holding the joy and speak the words you are feeling out loud to anyone or anything around you. I have experienced such grace in those moments when I feel connected to everyone and everything.

At my choice point, in the situation earlier, I could say that when I find myself condemning anything, no matter what it is, I am really looking for relief. It is a relief because now, in this moment, armed with new awareness, I know how to change that. In this moment, a new vibrational frequency has been established. Through the practice of deliberate blessing, you establish a new resonate frequency with the relationship you cherish and really want to have. Pay no attention to what *was*; let it go because it is irrelevant. You are all that matters, revealing you!

REACH FOR YOUR RADIANCE: A NEW
CHOICE POINT

You can continue to cycle in the familiar negative offenses and excuses, continue the blame game, or you can reach for your shining star. (Watch out for the familiar Yabbit, "that's easier said than done.")

You can begin with: "Wow, look at that! What a wonderful opportunity just opened up to me." Because I know that everything that happens in my life is a blessing, I take a deep breath, and look past the outer circumstance that just occurred. Blessing what has just occurred offers me leverage and an opportunity to see something greater at play. It feels so good to know I am worthy of happiness and joy. Balance and harmony point the way for me right now. I have nothing to do but just breathe. I am the breath of God, and my breath aligns me with All That Is.

If you are having a challenge shifting into joy, use the words in this chart to add positive emphasis to your blessings:

WORDS OF ENCOURAGEMENT

Adored	Abundant	Aligned	Allowing	Amazing
Awesome	Attractive	Appreciate	Balanced	Basking
Beaming	Beautiful	Belonging	Blessed	Blissful
Brilliant	Cheerful	Clear	Confident	Connected
Cooperative	Creative	Curious	Deliberate	Delicious
Delightful	Desiring	Empowered	Ease	Eager
Eternal	Exciting	Exciting	Excellent	Exhilarate
Exquisite	Expansion	Enthusiasm	Fortunate	Focused
Frisky	Fabulous	Flourishing	Forward-thinking	Free
Fulfilled	Genius	Gleeful	Glowing	Grateful
Generous	Gorgeous	Humorous	Hopeful	Healthy
Harmonious	Happy	Integrity	Inspired	Illuminated
Infinite	Interested	Inviting	Intriguing	Involved
Joyous	Jubilant	Knowing	Kind	Kingly
Kissable	Limitless	Luscious	Laughter	Lively
Loving	Luxurious	Light	Magnificent	Magical
Manifesting	Miracle	Natural	Nicer	Nimble
Open	Proud	Passion	Playful	Pleased
Prosperous	Present	Quiet	Queenly	Quintessential
Radiant	Reawakened	Ravishing	Refreshed	Relaxed
Released	Resonating	Romantic	Sensational	Sensuous
Spicy	Successful	Sure	Splendid	Sexy
Sunny	Tapped in Tuned in and Turned on	Trust	Thriving	Transcending
Thrilling	Thankful	Terrific	Tender	Tickled
Unconditional	Unified	Unique	Universal	Uplifting
Valued	Variety	Vibrant	Victorious	Visionary
Well-being	Welcoming	Whimsical	Winner	Worthy
Yes	Zany	Zesty	Zeal	

I love this exercise! It's easy to do and helps bring my awareness into a higher vibrational frequency.

1. Read over the list of words.

2. Pick out two or three that feel inspiring to you.

3. Use them in a sentence starting with: *It feels so good to be…*

4. Then move on to the next sentence: *I just love it when I feel…*

5. Then move on to the next sentence: *Gosh I really appreciate being…*

6. Give yourself at least 10 minutes of encouragement toward accepting your true, authentic, worthy, deserving self.

7. Now, with your desired thoughts in your mind, say: *As I live and breathe my desire to* [really feel joyful], *the excitement of having my dream just turns me on!*

There is power and leverage in alignment. No one can do it for you. Allow more uplifting and encouraging thoughts to flood your mind and with joy, speak them aloud.

We are all wondrous, lustrous, magnificent pearls open to the abundant joy of life through self-blessing.

The Pearl of Wisdom and the Act of Blessing

You are all joy. Joy is the essence of who you are!
Throughout the years, you may have hidden yourself away within
that craggy oyster shell.
Since your essence is pure joy, that grain of sand has created a
colossal, magnificent pearl.
This pearl, like the grain of sand that brought it forth, is endowed
with worthiness, beauty, intelligence, love, and knowing.
It is time now for the outer shell to give up resistance to allow
entrance to the treasure within.
Blessing relaxes the outer shell.
Blessing allows light.
Blessing reveals "The pearl of great price": You.
Blessing rings true within the heart of joy for all.
Blessing lifts the mystery of you, the pearl of wisdom that has
grown rich in experience, accumulating endless fortune, placing it
within your reach, becoming one with you.

JOY IS THE WAY

As the moments of blessing become more real to you, a depersonalizing of any situation takes effect, which, with a little time, will allow you to expand beyond "it," and see it from a new vantage point. This is leverage, and the relief you feel comes from being in this new vector point of attraction. The relief you feel is from continuing to appreciate yourself, and cherish the outcome you would really like to see happen. This is alignment at its best. In that exact moment, the resolve has already occurred, and the new reality is created.

Step into your new world, you are the pearl of great price. It is the reality you prefer powered by what you do want. Joy is the way.

Chapter 14

Into the Heart and Power of Joy

I AM THE ESSENCE OF PURE GOODNESS AND MY
GOODNESS HAS NOTHING TO DO WITH MY ACTIONS OR
THE ACTIONS OF ANYONE ELSE.

Within every thought, there is a bubble of joy calling us home! This little joy bubble longs to be found, and cries out to us in any way it can. As children, we recognized the voice of joy. Deep in our hearts, we knew that joy was the major factor in the vibrational fabric from which we were created.

As everything comes into alignment, can't you just hear the call to joy so loud that you are just not able to turn away?

The reactivating of joy is setting up a resonating frequency within the heart of humanity, and each one of us in particular, calling us into the expansion we have longed to experience, and each helped bring about. There is no turning back now, so let's make this ride an exhilarating one filled with excitement and joy.

A friend who read a draft of *Activate Joy* wrote, "AlixSandra has put together in this book what has taken some of us 30 years to learn." My own journey has been more than 30 years. It has been my gift to share with you my experiences and new processes to activate joy. From walking into your feelings to find your joy, to the Universal Laws, to getting to know your Yabbits and moving into the joy of deliberate creation, to basking and blessing and the Goodness Process, these are my treasures that I share with you.

JOY IS EVERYWHERE

Earlier in the book, we highlighted the work of Masaru Emoto and his extensive experiments with the blessing of water. His experiments suggest that human emotions alter the molecular structure of water crystals. In his book, *Hidden Messages in Water*, he gives us a visual excursion, photographic images into a world that shows the impact of our words, and how the emotions they carry affect the very structure of our being.

Joy Is Present Everywhere!

It comes forth from the light body and the emotional field of each
one of us.
Joy is the healer present in the cellular structures
of each one of us as well.
The power to change the world
into the world of our dreams
is within each and every one of us
as deliberate creators of our experience.

When I make a protein drink in the morning, it takes time to assemble my protein powder, frozen bananas, almond milk, and cinnamon. Each ingredient is selected and mixed in my drink with loving thoughts, and with the intention of blessing of my body. I have a favorite glass I like to use, and on the glass with a pen I write "Alignment, joy, joy, joy." Even the simple act of making my breakfast has become an act of deliberate creation.

We have new knowledge today that we have expanded into and are now ready to accept and integrate into our lives. If you have read this far, I know you have spent time and energy on yourself, clearing out old thought patterns, doing affirmations, and living in a more positive frame of mind. Using this knowledge to be a deliberate creator in your everyday life will tip the scales in favor of aligning completely with your birthright of joy so that joy becomes your dominant thought pattern.

The reason I call for alignment with joy is because I know; I trust that the power of joy will cause me to experience extraordinary things. I can build an empire, live to 150 years old and beyond, create masterpieces, write wonderful books, and sing like the angel I know myself to be.

IT TAKES TIME

Let me take you back to the peace event many years ago. After a year of loving and joyful hard work, we all fully expected that world peace would be a fact, a new way of life. We expected the great awakening to occur immediately within our world leaders and governments. Things didn't unfold in the exact way we anticipated, and an air of discouragement and pessimism invaded our Las Vegas spiritual community. The celebration was not long-lasting, and joy actually seemed hidden or hard to access for most of us. Eventually, the tight-knit spiritual community of Las Vegas unraveled, and most of us lost touch with each other. It would seem that the Yabbits had won. But not so! The paradigm shift I referred to was budding in the background, enlivened from the bulb buried deep within the heart of humanity. Something has shaken loose and many people around the globe are involved in so many ways. This in itself activates joy. Joy leads us to enlivened peace. I am so grateful I said yes to being the motivating force deliberately creating our Las Vegas gathering and experiencing that powerful moment in time.

What I have witnessed throughout these past 25 years since our event is a steady expansion of consciousness within myself. I see it in the world as more and more people seek to understand themselves in a better way. Our Yabbits will always be present to give us a kick in the pants, and force us to look to the blessing of life. Yabbits are not designed to cause grief. When your awareness is full, Yabbits can lead you to joy. Right now, today, this very moment, our challenge is to smile and look lovingly into the face of success, reach for the stars, and let ourselves get caught up in the vortex of the 2012 Alignment. It is here. It has already begun.

EXPERIENCING PEACE DURING CONFLICT

Here is an affirmation I worked on during a session with a couple facing a great challenge in their lives. The husband was scheduled to report to prison for a period of time. This was not just any old challenge, but one in which his freedom was being taken away. His wife was overwhelmed, wondering how she would fare while he was gone, which put her in her own prison of fear and anxiety. It looked as if their life was a hurricane offering nothing but destruction in its wake. So where is the joy? Where does deliberate creation come in? It certainly seems as if there is no free choice here, doesn't it? It is as if others are in control of his fate.

When I was in the sisterhood of Temple Ner Tamid, we hosted many luncheons with Hadassah, another women's organization within the Jewish community. I vividly recall listening to a guest speaker, a holocaust survivor recounting the details of her imprisonment and torture. Tears streamed down our cheeks as she, with a lilting joyous tone in her voice, told us how she survived. She sang under her breath all day and night. She counted sticks and bricks. When the guards grabbed her for their pleasure, she told them how wonderful they were. *Gasp! Gasp! Really?* She watched her friends and every family member go into the showers, never to return. As she began to conclude her talk, she was visibly lifted as her face beamed with joy. She was happy to be alive. Everything she touched, she cherished, excited to find the dawn in the morning light. Her parting words were these: "They could not break me because they could not control my thoughts." My husband's family came from Poland where many succumbed to the same fate. These words have been with me all these years, helping me realize the power of our own mind to deliberately shift realities no matter how it may look.

So during the session with the couple facing prison, as I talked, I found strength in different things for both of them, and I remembered this little woman. My experience told me to look for a common thread, a lifeline they could hold on to and lift themselves up with, and I suggested an affirmation universal enough, and yet, very specific to their needs. First we moved into a state of joy and found the entrance to the vortex of joy where all solutions are. We then, very deliberately, brought forth this statement: "My goodness is in my joy! Now the whole world celebrates my freedom as I move into my new life."

Here is a breakdown for you to follow why this statement was so imperative for the couple to accept:

- As we first entered the vortex of hope, we realized that this too shall pass and then made our statement with conviction: "My goodness is in my joy." This statement affirmed our birthright of abundance, our knowing of our eternal worthiness.

- "Now the whole world…" In essence, we stated that in this present moment, we draw on the vast consciousness of our human family to be with us.

- "…celebrates my freedom…" From continent to continent, from sea to shining sea, the voice of freedom does ring out from the hearts of all people everywhere. This is our God-given right to free choice.

- "…as I move into my new life." Years ago, while I was preparing to officiate at a funeral, my friend and mentor Jesus offered me this option…consider the words of this Psalm for birth and death. Now it also seems quite appropriate for this situation. So as I move into my new life, "…surely goodness and mercy shall follow me all the days of my life." (Psalm 23:6)

These words are as relevant in our lives today as ever. When we consider using them as a deliberate creator, the potential exists that a critical shift can happen. A shift from agony to hope, then from hope to joy, from condemned to blessed. So blessed, you can actually allow a miracle to show up right now in this very moment.

The peace event changed my life for the better, and now I realize as I write these words, this event opened the vortex of creative potential for me and many others.

There is peace in the world for those who choose peace.

And that is the operative word—*choose.*

To be at peace requires that we actively embrace the differences of others with enthusiasm. When we allow others the freedom to choose a life path, even if they are choosing pain and suffering, without urging them to conform to our way of life, we offer them the greatest power of all—the choice to activate the joy within them. This is the ultimate act of grace, an opportunity to practice true generosity.

There will always be teachers, there will always be setbacks; both are critical elements in the human journey. After a lifetime of study and experiences with both, my conclusion is simply that the brass ring or gold standard is joy activated. Joy is the only thing worth reaching for. Once you access joy, everything lines up; therefore everything else is irrelevant.

CREATING NEW THOUGHT FORMS

Up until now, humanity as a whole has been living in a crystallized state; by that I mean we have been living with thought forms that seem to be set in stone. Thought forms are ideas of certainty built up over time by many people simply accepting the idea to be true. These were unconscious agreements that few of us were aware of, and fewer still as individuals could seemingly do anything about them. From the human potential movement of the 1970s and 1980s, to the spiritual revolution of the 1990s, to the present time, this crystallization of thought forms has slowly been in the process of breaking down and reorganizing itself. Outdated ways of thinking, and the illusions connected with them, are fading as the magnetic pull towards a higher standard becomes even more powerful.

Each generation expands consciousness so that the generation yet to be born can experience the expansion. And now, this exponential explosion of joy is reaching out in ways we just can't imagine. We are in new and uncharted territory.

This revolution touches you when the desire to find your own truth becomes stronger than your will to live within the belief patterns of your parents' generation. The desire has become so strong within the fabric of the world soul that it has shifted the heart of humanity. Today, many once esoteric spiritual principles and concepts have become part of the mainstream.

Television programs such as *The Oprah Winfrey Show* have grown from this consciousness. Oprah's spirit and the information she has shared has touched and shifted millions of people. On a grand scale, she has offered hope, and more importantly, she has offered her viewers ways to develop their own self-awareness, which is making a difference.

Joy has opened a vortex that raised and expanded conscious awareness for people to follow their hearts and find new precious meaning in their lives. Huge chasms of indifference are bridged and the gaps are rapidly closing. Each day, freedom in as many different ways as there are people, is deliberately reclaimed and realized.

Continued spiritual development takes commitment and focus. It takes grounding and it takes continued reflection long after the program/workshop/class is over or you finish reading this book. It requires trust in your true nature, and faith in your personal truth that may not look like anything you've ever seen before. For many, the tendency might be to fall back into old familiar ways when, after this point of development, nothing looks familiar. Seeking security, seeking safety, seeking a soft place to land. Egads! Actually, nothing feels safe.

Programs such as Inner Focus are here to go the distance with people, to provide the long-term tools that allow the natural flow of consciousness to integrate and stabilize, if that is your path. We use these tools to mature from our wounds, and move from the place that seeks safety to a place of accountability. Your guidance will lead you right into the perfect place for you to align with your true desires. There are many paths and they all lead to the same place: home.

ENERGY FOLLOWS CONSCIOUSNESS

Deliberately Choose to Follow Your Heart

When we consistently make choices from the joy within our heart, we learn to live in the flow of the moment, elastic and accessible. Accountability says, "If I created it, I can change it."

The truth is, when we activate joy, everything relaxes and flows in union with the vortex of the heart (which contains the pathways of unconditional love, nonjudgment, and equality).

Initiations can feel like earthquakes and hurricanes. They can be cataclysmic and life-changing. These are natural parts of our evolutionary process. If you think you are alone in this process, just ask a friend.

Look back at an active hurricane season. When one storm came right after another, a relentless breaking down of old realities, of old ways of thinking, occurred. The Middle East turmoil and the elections in the United States have what to do with joy? They give me a challenge to be in joy no matter what. I have the power of the freedom to be and act from my center no matter what is breaking down around me, no matter who is trying to hold on to outdated ways of thinking, no matter who is trying to control and manipulate my life. When you can hold a vision for your own truth and make that your focused reality in the midst of chaos, that is a moment to be treasured...

Source is expanding and evolving, and we are all a part of Source and part of this event. Denial that a massive change is occurring within humanity is no longer an option. This is an initiation into the heart. This means quite simply that we are ready to be finished with a power-driven world of material acquisitions and conquests, pain and suffering, and shift into a more heart-centered world. This will be a world of individuals who make the conscious decision to come from the place of compassion and humility, and reject the past pattern of power over others and manipulation of their reality. Whether you are a waitress, minister, or world leader, this initiation will bring you into your heart. This is the place of joy. This initiation dares you to know yourself and your energy, as you put yourself in a place of choosing and stay grounded in your truth.

Are you ready for the responsibility of your heart? Have you prepared well for this time?

Don't be scared, and don't shrink from the awesome moment you are entering into that you created for yourself.

HIGH LIGHT, HIGH JOY

Hidden within your heart is the spark of creative genius that is pushing through those upper layers of resistance. This spark or light may still remain to illuminate the light of your True Self in human form. This light is your essence, the place where your true power emanates from. The awesome moment when you stand on the brink of the paradigm shift and fearlessly fall to merge into the vortex of the heart, your joy will cradle you and gently point you in the direction of happiness and fulfillment.

The grandmothers and grandfathers of ancient wisdom know this place well. They worked to prepare each one of us through their individual lives to meet this challenge, to ride the whale, to hear the whispers, to stand tall and emerge from this vision quest of life as a human awakened and enlightened. The shadows are receding quickly and without protest in the dawn of this new day.

Walking out of the ring of fire and into that place of deep knowing, we are secure and confident. This process is creating a more deeply intimate relationship with your very own Source energy. Feel the strength of a hundred hurricanes moving you forward, creatively building new realities, new bridges, and new worlds with excitement and resolve. Joy activated has become a crane lifting 10-ton boulders with ease.

The heart is both the way and the destination, for within the heart is a great template that wants to be activated so that each brand new day is deliberately created from the heart of compassion and generosity. It is Source that has brought you to this moment, even to experience reading this book and receiving this gift. Your willingness to ride the wave has carried you through to this point. Trust that a co-creative effort has prepared you for this initiation. You have earned this honor, you have earned great respect, and now is the time for you to be a leader in this time of great change.

Now, rise to the occasion and accept the responsibility that is required to make the choices that will consciously and deliberately create the world we truly want. What was once unfamiliar is now an exciting new prospect and leading-edge adventure. What was once feared now presents itself as an opening into a new creative experience. Open up, and welcome your neighbors into the sanctuary of your heart.

The initiation process requires a willingness to receive your birthright. The initiation process tests your strength, purpose, and resolve. It requires making a choice for life, integrity, and celebration. This is a golden opportunity; the door will remain open now, beckoning you to live fully in the frequency you and I collectively create. This palpable vibration holds the purest ascension frequencies of equality, abundance, acceptance, and divine love.

Once our birthright is embraced, the worn-out ego world of separateness, judgment, dualism, condemnation, domination, and limitation ebbs away and disappears…as it must. The path of initiation has brought us together for a profound reason: to realize our self as Masters of Divine Light and Love, and to live into that truth now.

GOODNESS

In *Activate Joy*, you learned how to do the Goodness Process, and now it is time to do the Goodness Process for your ascension. This process was revealed as a practice instructing the body to release the ego world and to embrace the spirit of oneness.

I am the essence of pure goodness and my goodness has nothing to do with my actions or the actions of anyone else.

That statement, along with the practices you have learned, will change your perception of everything. Alignment with your own divine mystical nature inevitably occurs. We have each diligently prepared ourselves for this transition and are ready to put all the pieces together. As we deal with the changes in our world and the changes in our own lives, we begin to realize that something most profound is at hand. Something is bringing us to the edge of life as we have known it, and it excites every cell in our being with anticipation. Life beyond the ego world is exhilarating. I encourage you to gracefully rise to the life-changing occasion being presented. Join me in this quantum experience.

EPILOGUE

LOVE IS THE ANSWER.

Much of what I have shared with you is autobiographical in nature. I have allowed myself the deep pleasure of honoring my life by inviting you along on the many paths I have taken to find self-love, introducing you to the people I met along the way and sharing how they have changed the course of my quest. My students, friends, and family have been amazing and I bask in the memories of how they showed up to be cooperative components. They have used the keys I have been given to make their lives more joyful.

As I complete this writing, I look back through the years that it took me to get to this moment in time and I clearly see that many of my greatest teachers were also non-physical. Somewhere deep within me I felt that I could trust what was being said by these teachers just a little more.

I believe the non-physical energies that I have first-hand knowledge of transmitted their messages through corridors of unconditional love, bringing their messages more to our hearts than our minds. Each one gave hope for the future, empowering our own ability to reach deep within and bring our own unique message to others on the wings of that same stream of love. While in that stream of love, you are in a state of being that allows the communication to flow through to you with ease. When my teacher Jesus visited, he gave me the powerful pieces of insight to assimilate into my life, including, "I am in the world, but not of the world."

Love develops intuition. Intuition uses feelings to point the way to more expansion, greater knowledge, and deeper wisdom, which benefit us greatly. Love is joy activated.

Unconditional Love Is the Key

Unconditional love is just that—love without conditions. Unconditional love is the foundation of blessing within the paradigm shift I have discussed. In great masses, humanity is moving away from wanting power over other people to valuing the empowerment of one another. "The meek shall inherit the Earth." People want their freedom and are unwilling to live under the rule of the Yabbit world any longer.

Following my inner call to greatness, I founded a school of energy healing in 1994. I remember someone asked me if I had a charter, and who was underwriting me. Exactly who was giving me permission to do such a thing as creating a school? Taken off guard, I clearly remember my answer: "I guess I gave myself permission. After all, aren't you my monitors? If I don't meet your needs, you won't come back." That was an innocent statement and now when I look back on the truth of it, it helps me stay in integrity. The inner guidance I followed was not looking to any other institution or group for approval— my passion and desire were the only approval necessary. The follow-through was easy because it was my destiny and all the "cooperative components" were assembled to make it so.

In my first school catalogue I wrote, "You have to love yourself before you can love others." That statement came from an inner knowing that was never taught to me; instead it came to me. Unconditional love is, first and foremost, loving yourself unconditionally. Never condemn yourself for anything, rather, learn from what that relationship had to offer and quickly move on. When you stop condemning yourself, it will never occur to you to condemn anyone else. The words you speak and the feelings you project are then unconditional.

Spiritual maturity is understanding that we are all in this together. This lifetime that you are experiencing was deliberately chosen because of the excitement of the day. Now, at this stage of awareness, our self-focus need not be harsh. There is nothing to protect or defend against. Ease and flow are the order of the day. As the powerful teaching on the Law of Attraction is now becoming widespread in our culture, it is also important to realize that the energy of unconditional love is surging beneath the surf. This is the time of alignment as we take our existence beyond the beyond.

As I write this section, a woman stopped to remark on how lovely it has been for her to see me writing every day in this magnificent spot overlooking the bay here in Australia. As we talked and shared a moment, I asked her if she was here with the conference that I noticed earlier. She said, "Yes, they were here creating new strategies for their company." As I reflect on that gentle woman, I realize that is exactly what I am doing—creating new strategies. She reflected perfectly the very intent of my writing, a cooperative component sent from the source of me to let me know I am right on track. Now I take time to be in deep appreciation for this woman and her company, and hold her with unconditional love. I am aware and deliberately conscious of the true meaning of that brief encounter. As a result, it has given me a deeper perspective on my purpose. I also realize that I love the quiet beauty of nature, and I feel aligned with myself here without any distractions to tempt me away from my joy.

Basking in the Activate Joy Paradigm

As we move beyond the paradigm shift, we are being collectively taken on a joy ride. Hang on—it will be a very fun adventure. To arrive at this fantastic opportunity, each of us has been on a journey of preparation so that we could be ready to embrace all the new things that are unfolding for us. Teachers such as Jesus, Seth, Bashar, and countless others opened the way for me and shined the light on my path. This golden age has arrived for all of us to experience what it feels like to be humans experimenting and playing with our new awareness of joy in our lifetime.

The formula for the paradigm shift is so simple that it often has us wondering, "Wait a minute…could it be that easy?" Basically, when enough people are doing the same thing, because we are all connected, everyone consciously shifts. That is the paradigm shift stated simply. Have you heard that wonderful poem about the child who picked up one starfish and gently put it back in the ocean? In the poem the beach was littered with hundreds of starfish and the parent asked why the child was doing this, because there was no way he could help all the starfish. The child replied that he had made a difference for that one little starfish and that was enough for him. You are the starfish tossed back into an ocean of unconditional love that starts a process of the expansion that activates joy. I deliberately choose to live joy every day. I encourage you to realize that the most powerful thing you can do in every moment is to choose joy. Know when you are off the mark and make the shift into joy your greatest priority. When you choose joy, you become the embodiment of joy that naturally affects your reality as well as the reality of others. Your joy is a flint that creates a spark that ignites the fire of unconditional love that subsequently creates more joy.

This book was written because I activated joy. My intention is for you to cherish the love I give to you through these pages, add it to your treasure chest, use the tools, and pay it forward when you are ready because you are a very important link in the chain of love. You matter more than words can say. I encourage you to believe in yourself and follow your heart because love is always the answer.

Thank you for making this journey with me.

AlixSandra Parness

October 2011

Appendix A:

Power Blessings

Living Your Life Beyond Limitations Takes Practice

In this section, I have given you several highly potent blessings for real-life challenges that you can use to instantly shift your point of attraction from negative to positive. These blessings can be used as you practice your desire to live in the higher frequency of joy. They are especially powerful when you read them aloud to yourself.

Practicing blessing everything, even that which seems difficult to bless, always makes you feel better. Every time you bless, you also align yourself with love.

The power from blessing brings freedom and freedom activates joy.

Over/undereating or substance abuse

There was a time that I could not see myself as separate from others. I used to look for anything to numb the empty pain from the unhappiness I continued to feel, until one magnificent day when I was blessed by the angel within me, and I woke up. I woke up to the realization that I am the blessing of me. There is no substitution for the connection I have with all that I am. There is no substance that could ever substitute for the power of the joy I feel as I take control of my own life. I am the blessing of me now and always, lifted into the freedom of unlimited success.

Codependency

There is a blessing in knowing who I am—a blessing in the recognition that when it comes right down to it, I am the only one living my life. I am willing to take the steps necessary to allow others their freedom to make their own choices, and as I do, I expand in my own freedom to live my life as I want to, easily asking for what I want, and making choices that bring me joy, time after time.

Grief

I bless my grief as I feel the loss of someone dear to me. I hold in my heart all the blessings we shared as pleasant and joyous. At the same time, I reach for the strength to notice my life continually unfolding before me. Life is stopping for nothing because life is like a fast-moving river carrying me forward, always drawing me into my next experience. Today I release resistance. Today I embrace appreciation for what was and allow myself to feel anticipation for what is to come.

Crisis

This too shall pass. I feel joy coming from my alignment with my true and deep self. I allow my vision to awaken the knowledge of well-being that is all around me. I know exactly what to do. I know exactly what to say. Everything always works out for me and I can trust that in this instance there is a point of power showing itself to me. I bless all that is happening and hold the vision of perfect right action in all ways.

Confusion

I bless the confusion I feel in this moment and in blessing this I begin to rise above it. I feel the relief of clarity reaching for me. As I trust myself, I align with the best and highest within me, and I begin to feel better. I can focus on the sun as it beams its way through the clouds and revel in its beauty. My solutions are always in front of me and I allow myself the time I need to stop and smell the roses, to clear my thoughts, and release myself into the knowing that all is well. As I do, my answers become crystal clear, and activate the joy of clarity.

Decision

I stand here within the blessings of choice and free will. As I ponder the ideas that are before me, I am noticing what draws my attention, what lifts my heart, and what fills me with pleasure, and so my decision becomes clearer. I trust my ability to make decisions. I follow the path I am drawn to and know that there are other decisions still waiting for me. As I believe in myself, and the direction my joy points me in, my decisions become exhilarating moments of creativity.

Health

I am blessed with a body of infinite intelligence living in a world blessed with an abundance of well-being. I love training my thoughts to reflect the joy of life and the exuberance of living. My thoughts flow with power from my inner self filled with strength, stamina, and good health. I believe in myself and I know that as I find things that please and uplift me, I feel healthy. It is in these moments the cells of my body joyously celebrate their good health.

Change

I notice that everything is always moving. Ideas and desires shift as I expand my thoughts of who I am. I am growing and I am excited to see what is in store for me. I feel the blessing from my creative nature, causing me to reach for greater and greater acceptance of my own value. I am worthy of having a great and fulfilling experience that embraces my talents and lifts my heart.

Money

I am blessed to live in a world of abundance. There is so much that brings me pleasure that I am willing to count my blessings with each wonderful thing. Sometimes I feel like the most fortunate person in the world. I am showered with so much love from so many people; even my dog loves me and wants to please me. The better I feel, the more I want to bless everything in my life. So I bless my abundance as I feel money easily coming to me. I release any impatience I might be holding onto and allow feelings of expectancy and eagerness for what is coming. All I have to do right now is align my good-feeling thoughts with the sensation of freedom. I am having fun watching my expansion into financial wealth and I so appreciate these good feelings. I bless the universe, as it yields to me according to my thoughts of abundance and freedom.

Relationships

I am blessed to know that I am growing and learning that all of my relationships are drawn to me by me. I realize that only I can control me and how I feel in any given circumstance. I can never control the thoughts or actions of anyone else so I willingly release those old ideas and now embrace new joyful ideas. I just love being with someone who knows who he/she is. I am the happiest when we can notice how much we have in common and talk for hours and never get bored. When I think of this person, my heart leaps and I feel anticipation for what is to come. As I continue to bless the highest and best I have to offer, I know that is all that can come to me. My relationships have reached a higher standard through the blessing of who I am.

Insecurities

Sometimes I feel fear about doing something and instead of allowing my own inner guidance to show me the right path to take, I ask others for advice. Often, as they express I "should" follow their advice, I feel disempowered. Today I take my power back. I empower myself to think my own thoughts and feel my own feelings. I bless the world I have created and know that I am secure and loved for who I am. There is nothing wrong with me, I can't fail and I can't really make a mistake even though it might seem like I can. I bless myself as a worthy, deserving person with my birthright of joy in this universe; I claim it, I accept it, I am secure in the knowing of it; and I allow all things good and very good to come to me.

Commitment

I trust who I am and who I am becoming. This feeling is so exciting to me, it is easy to be committed to me. I am committed to being the best I can be in each and every situation. I sense the blessing in commitment and in that I am more deeply connected with my inner being. Hope is like a wave that springs eternal and so I am committed to knowing both sides of the wave and to always trusting myself to follow my joy. I can't ever get it wrong and I can never get it all done because there will always be another wave to greet me. The more I train my thoughts and feelings in the power of commitment to my joy, I experience the ease and flow of accomplishing everything I desire and more.

Separation or divorce

Relationships are blessings that allow me to see where I am. I recognize myself as a vibrational being expanding and growing constantly. My marriage (relationship) has been a great blessing to me in many ways and I will always hold dear to my heart the many blessings that have come from this relationship. I now bless the parting of our ways and recognize the new frequency calling both of us into new adventures. I welcome my new opportunity to discover more of who I am, expressing my creative spirit more fully. All is well. All is blessed.

Self-image

I love who I am! Each morning I am excited to see what the day will bring, who I will meet, and how I will sound as I greet each one. I love to feel my skin as I shower and get ready for my day. My body is perfect just the way it is and I bless myself.

I bless all that I have to offer each moment of the day. I am loved. I am blessed with vitality and self-assurance. I enjoy the ecstasy of living every wonderful moment, even when it does not feel so good, because I know how to bring myself back into good-feeling thoughts. I am a beautiful person, handsome, and lovely. I admire myself and appreciate where I am going.

Sexuality

Sex is wonderful, my ecstasy aligns me with the power of life-giving joy. I feel good about my sexual pleasures and I bless the body and soul of me. I belong to myself and when I choose to share my joy sexually it is always a happy experience. I choose because I now have the awareness to be in a place that feels good to me.

Negative thoughts

Every time I look at this specific problem a committee of Yabbits begins to yammer in my head. So today, I will bless those negative thoughts and choose to see the positive intentions behind them. As I begin to feel better, I will look for something easy to bless, such as the cool wind coming off the lake or the sunshine peeking through the leaves of a tree. I bask in the ease and flow of the moment and know that my world is bringing me into a feeling of harmony. I don't have to pay attention to anything but feeling good and free right now, and so it is.

For the dying

My dearest, what a wonderful life you have lived. Look at all the blessings you have bestowed in the world. You have done everything right and there is nothing left undone. As you release all resistance right now, feel the freedom of joy lifting you, ready to whisk you away. I love you and my love will be with you always as yours is always with me. In celebration right now, I sing you a song of the beloved you are, my melody coming from the depth of your heartstrings.

Animals

I marvel at the animal kingdom on planet Earth. I find joy in the diversity of all shapes and sizes. I feel deeply blessed by all these beings because they know who they are. There is no confusion within them; there is only the desire to live and enjoy their life. I am blessed with their unconditional love and I deeply appreciate all animals for their reflection of complete self-acceptance.

World

With enthusiasm, I embrace differences and I bless the world and all of the life forms that create a magnificent tapestry of teeming life, creating life. I easily bless the varied belief systems and bless each person as he or she discovers day by day the love and joy from which he or she is made. I love living with people who share different ideas and cultures, and ponder how I feel within their thoughts. I am enthusiastic as I experience the kaleidoscope of wonder in the world.

Family and the people we choose to call our family

Family is the greatest blessing one can embrace, even when family feels distant or disconnected. The idea of family creates a powerful place for me to grow and expand. I explore the truth of who I really am through their diversity of perceptions, opinions, ideas, and the directions they want me to take. I appreciate the power of family, even when we disagree. Family requires my strength of self to be me with joy, love, and acceptance. I love my family, and I bless all families. I bless the love and the reaching for more love in so many diverse ways.

Love

Love blesses me in everything I do. Love never judges or criticizes me. Love allows my free will to abound. I am made from love. Love is who I am. As I bless my life and the world I create day by day, love expands me and brings me more love. As I reach for joy, love answers me. As I reach for my power, love answers me. Love blesses my life and I, in turn, bless life with my love.

I am the essence of pure goodness.
My goodness has nothing to do with my actions or the actions of anyone else.

Appendix B:

Recommended Reading

Anka, Darryl. *Bashar—Blueprint for Life: A Message from Our Future.* Seattle, Wash.: New Solutions Publications, 1990.

Brennan, Barbara. *Hands of Light: A Guide to Healing Through the Human Energy Field.* New York: Bantam Books, 1987.

———. *Light Emerging: The Journey of Personal Healing.* New York: Bantam Books, 1993.

Dyer, Wayne. *Excuses Be Gone! How to Change Lifelong, Self-Defeating Thinking Habits.* Carlsbad, Calif.: Hay House, 2011.

Emoto, Masaru. *The Hidden Messages in Water.* Hillsboro, Ore.: Beyond Words Publications, 2004.

Ferrini, Paul. *Love Without Conditions: Reflections of the Christ Mind.* Greenfield, Mass.: Heart Ways Press, 1995.

Gandee, Lee Raus. *Strange Experiences: The Autobiography of a Hexemeister.* Upper Saddle River, N.J.: Prentice Hall Publications, 1971.

Hicks, Esther, and Jerry Hicks. *The Amazing Power of Deliberate Intent: Living the Art of Allowing.* Carlsbad, Calif.: Hay House, 2006.

———. *Ask and It Is Given: Learning to Manifest Your Desires.* Carlsbad, Calif.: Hay House, 2005.

———. *The Law of Attraction: The Basics of the Teachings of Abraham.* Carlsbad, Calif.: Hay House, 2006.

———. *The Vortex: Where the Law of Attraction Assembles All Cooperative Relationships.* Carlsbad, Calif.: Hay House, 2009.

Price, John Randolph. *The Planetary Commission.* Boerne, Texas: Quartus Foundation, 1984. Reprinted as *The Workbook for Self-Mastery: A Course of Study on the Divine Reality.* Carlsbad, Calif.: Hay House, 1998.

Roberts, Jane. *The Magical Approach: Seth Speaks About the Art of Creative Living.* San Rafael, Calif.: Amber-Allen Publishing, 1995.

———. *The Nature of Personal Reality: Specific, Practical Techniques for Solving Everyday Problems and Enriching the Life You Know.* San Rafael, Calif.: Amber-Allen Publishing, 1994.

———. *The Seth Material.* Manhasset, N.Y.: New Awareness Network, 2001.

———. *The World View of Paul Cezanne: A Psychic Interpretation.* Upper Saddle River, N.J.: Prentice Hall Publications, 1982.

Stone Hal, and Sidra Stone. *Partnering: A New Kind of Relationship.* Novato, Calif.: New World Library, 2000.

Stone, Hal, Sidra Stone, and Shakti Gawain. *Embracing Ourselves: The Voice Dialogue Manual.* Novato, Calif.: New World Library, 1998.

Appendix C:

Inner Focus Certified Teachers and Practitioners

Through joy, healing and upliftment are activated and the mysteries of life are resolved, thus healing the heart of humanity, one heart at a time.

Inner Focus Programs offer a beautiful combination of teaching and experiential work, which naturally flows with group energy. Dr. AlixSandra and her international community of passionate Inner Focus faculty members teach empowering sessions offered through her Inner Focus programs.

Our expanding universe is calling us into our greatness and power. You can become an activator of well-being that calls forth the natural you, and vibrationally transform your life.

Through Inner Focus programs, you will discover dynamic tools for upliftment and alignment that are practical, easily understood, and can be used right away for yourself and others. Your essence fully awakens through the empowerment of your eternal nature. You will enter your vortex of joy with health, happiness, and wholeness as your partners and you bring your world with you!

Inner Focus is a life-enhancing experience of empowerment. Your transformation will be immediate. The results are positively delicious!

The following list includes active teachers and practitioners from the Inner Focus School that have completed the four-year certification program. AlixSandra honors them for their passion, joy, and support. Search this list to find one near you or visit *www.activatejoy.com* and send a request to connect with a practitioner near you.

USA

Cindy Capitani, CAEH, MMS, San Antonio, Tex.

Barbara May Duman, CAEH, MMS, Riverwoods, Ill.

Joanne Eggenberger, CAEH , Oconomowoc, Wis.

Eric Ehrke, LCSW, LMFT, AEH, Milwaukee, Wis.

Victoria Grey, CAEH, MMS, Taos, N.M.

Arleen Hollenhorst, RN, HN-BC, CAEH, Menomonee Falls, Wis.

Dr. Russ Jackman, DC, CAEH, DD, Little Rock, Ark.

Andra Larson, CAEH, MMS, Swannanoa, N.C.

Jeanne Lee Rogers, CAEH, MMS, Barrington, Ill. and Crosslake, Minn.

Kenneth Mason, CAEH, Chicago, Ill.

Sheilana Massey, CAEH, DD, Bokeelia, Fla.

Laurel Mamet, CAEH, MMS, Fletcher, N.C.

Diane Therese Miller, M.Ed., L.Ac., CAEH, MMS, Chicago, Ill.

Judith Nolan, CAEH, Marco Island, Fl. and Evanston, Ill.

Kathleen Pape, CAEH, Madison, Wis.

Cindy Schultz, MA, LP, MMS, CAEH, MMS, St. Paul, Minn.

Marjorie Schramm, RN, MS, CAEH, McFarland, Wis.

Courtney Shimenetto, CAEH, Chicago, Ill.

Stacy Steinberg, CAEH, Northbrook, Ill.

Sunfire (Robert Kazmayer), CAEH, Greenwich, N.Y.

Linda F. Westphal-Buth, M.M.S., CAEH, Cedar Grove, Wis.

Canada

Michelle Atterby, CAEH, Victoria, British Columbia

Mitsi Rose Cardinal, CAEH, Chelsea, Quebec

Dr. Steve Hudson, CAEH, D.MT., P.Eng., D.Ac., Cornwall, Ontario

Rev. Dr. Wendy Hudson, DD, C.D.W., C.S.H., Cornwall, Ontario

Shirley Lennox, CAEH, MMS, Ottawa, Ontario

Murray Lennox, CAEH, MMS, Ottawa, Ontario

Tanya Lennox, MSc, CAEH, Whitby, Ontario

Ana Mayorga, CAEH, Ottawa, Ontario

Alisa Pfeifle, CAEH, Waterloo, Ontario

Des Sagragao, CAEH, Toronto, Ontario

Marcia Wolter, CAEH, Quadra Island, British Columbia

INDEX

About the Author

Dr. AlixSandra Parness, DD, is a dedicated healer who has spent a lifetime refining her clairvoyant, channeling, and teaching abilities, as well her ability to stay in a constant state of joy.

To polish her natural abilities, she trained in a wide variety of modalities, from working with psychic surgeons, to studying with Jane Roberts, to becoming one of Barbara Brennan's first students, to being a senior faculty member and national coordinator for the School of Energy Mastery in Sedona, Arizona. As an ordained minister and Doctor of Divinity, she led and founded churches in Las Vegas, Nevada. In 1994, Dr. Parness founded and directed the Inner Focus School for Soul Directed Advanced Energy Healing as an international vehicle for attaining personal enlightenment and world peace.

Her personal journey led her to an even greater vision of world service. Dr. Parness is a passionate activator of well-being with the ability to find, hold, and lift individual and group energy and stabilize the group. Her connection with the realms of divine love opens space for spontaneous healings and enlightened information to come that uplifts the hearts of individuals and reveals soul lessons in a gentle, firm, and empowering way. It's impossible to experience this woman without being forever touched and moved into heightened joy.

As a teacher of teachers, in her extensive workshops and healing school, Dr. Parness has trained several thousand students, many of whom today have their own expanding networks and now touch thousands more. A dynamic and unforgettable presence, she teaches through seminars and teleconferences, and at special events held across the United States and Canada.

She resides in Las Vegas, Nevada. She invites you to visit her at ActivateJoy.com.

About AlixSandra Parness's Inner Focus Advanced

Energy Healing School

Founded by Dr. AlixSandra Parness, DD

Directed by Laurel Mamet, MMS

Our expanding universe is calling us into our greatness and power. You can become the activator of well-being that is the natural you and vibrationally transform your life. Through Inner Focus, you will discover dynamic tools for upliftment and alignment that are practical, easily understood, and can be used right away for yourself and others. Your essence is fully awakened to the power of your eternal nature. You will enter your vortex of joy with health, happiness, and wholeness as your partners.

Through the birthright of joy, your higher consciousness is activated and the mysteries of life are revealed, thus healing the heart of humanity, one heart at a time. The Inner Focus Healing School offers an in-depth combination of teaching and experiential work, resulting in personal healing and spiritual mastery. You will be fully qualified as a healing professional, to set up a practice and explore the expanding realms of energy medicine. The empowering classes offered through The Healing School are taught by Regional Director Laurel Mamet, with specific sessions led by Founder and International Director Dr. AlixSandra Parness.

The Inner Focus School is a living, breathing, regenerative teaching. Your transformation will be immediate. The results are positively delicious!

Healing modalities:

- ❧ Mastering the art of joy, living your life beyond limitations
- ❧ Establishing higher states of consciousness
- ❧ Universal laws and how they apply
- ❧ A.R.T.: Inner Focus Alignment Resonance Technique
- ❧ 2-point hands on healing
- ❧ Clairvoyance training
- ❧ Higher brain activation
- ❧ The Art of Intentional Blessing
- ❧ Soul-centered/client-centered healing
- ❧ Advanced energetic anatomy

You will experience:

- ❧ Communicating with your Higher Self and Source
- ❧ Inner focus, meditation, and movement
- ❧ Transformation of core issues
- ❧ Creating your unique reality and living it
- ❧ Living from your passionate heart
- ❧ Manifestation of your creative genius
- ❧ Self-empowerment and wisdom
- ❧ Meditation, music, and laughter

For more information about AlixSandra Parness's Inner Focus Advanced Energy Healing School, please visit *www.innerfocus.info*

Contact AlixSandra:

Phone: (800) 600-8283

E-mail: innerfocus1@me.com

Contact Laurel:

Phone: (828) 650-0920

E-mail: wiselight@gmail.com